Andy Griffiths started having adventures the moment he was born, and has been having them (and writing about them) ever since.

You can find out more at www.andygriffiths.com.au

Bill Hope accidentally drew himself into existence with a crayon at an early age and has been drawing ever since.

You can find out more at www.billhope.com.au

ALSO BY ANDY GRIFFITHS
(illustrated by Terry Denton)

The 13-Storey Treehouse
The 26-Storey Treehouse
The 39-Storey Treehouse
The 52-Storey Treehouse
The 65-Storey Treehouse
The 78-Storey Treehouse
The 91-Storey Treehouse
The 104-Storey Treehouse
The 117-Storey Treehouse
The 130-Storey Treehouse
The 143-Storey Treehouse
The 156-Storey Treehouse
The 169-Storey Treehouse
Treehouse Tales
The Treehouse Fun Book 1, 2 and 3
The Bumper Treehouse Fun Book
The Treehouse Joke Book 1 and 2
Who's Who and What's Where in the Treehouse
Just Tricking!
Just Annoying!
Just Stupid!
Just Crazy!
Just Disgusting!
Just Shocking!
Just Macbeth!
Just Doomed!
The Cat on the Mat is Flat
The Big Fat Cow That Goes Kapow
What Bumosaur is That?
What Body Part is That?
Once Upon a Slime: 45 fun ways to get writing . . . FAST!

(illustrated by Bill Hope)

You & Me and the Land of Lost Things
You & Me and the Peanut Butter Beast

ANDY GRIFFITHS

BESTSELLING AUTHOR OF THE TREEHOUSE SERIES

LET'S GO!

ILLUSTRATED BY
BILL HOPE

PAN
Pan Macmillan Australia

Pan Macmillan acknowledges the Traditional Custodians of Country throughout Australia and their connections to lands, waters and communities. We pay our respect to Elders past and present and extend that respect to all Aboriginal and Torres Strait Islander peoples today. We honour more than sixty thousand years of storytelling, art and culture.

First published 2026 in Pan by Pan Macmillan Australia Pty Ltd
1 Market Street, Sydney, New South Wales, Australia, 2000
Reprinted 2026

A catalogue record for this book is available from the National Library of Australia

Internal design by i2i Design
Typeset in 13 / 16 Kepler Std by i2i Design
Printed by IVE
Ed and Ted and *Ducks in Trucks* were adapted from stories that first appeared in *The Cat on the Mat is Flat* (2006) and *Brave Dave* first appeared in *The Big Fat Cow That Goes Kapow* (2008).

Contents

1 AMAZiNG ADVeNTUReS 1

2 ANIMAL TALES 39

WAS THAT AN ELEPHANT?

WHEEEEE!

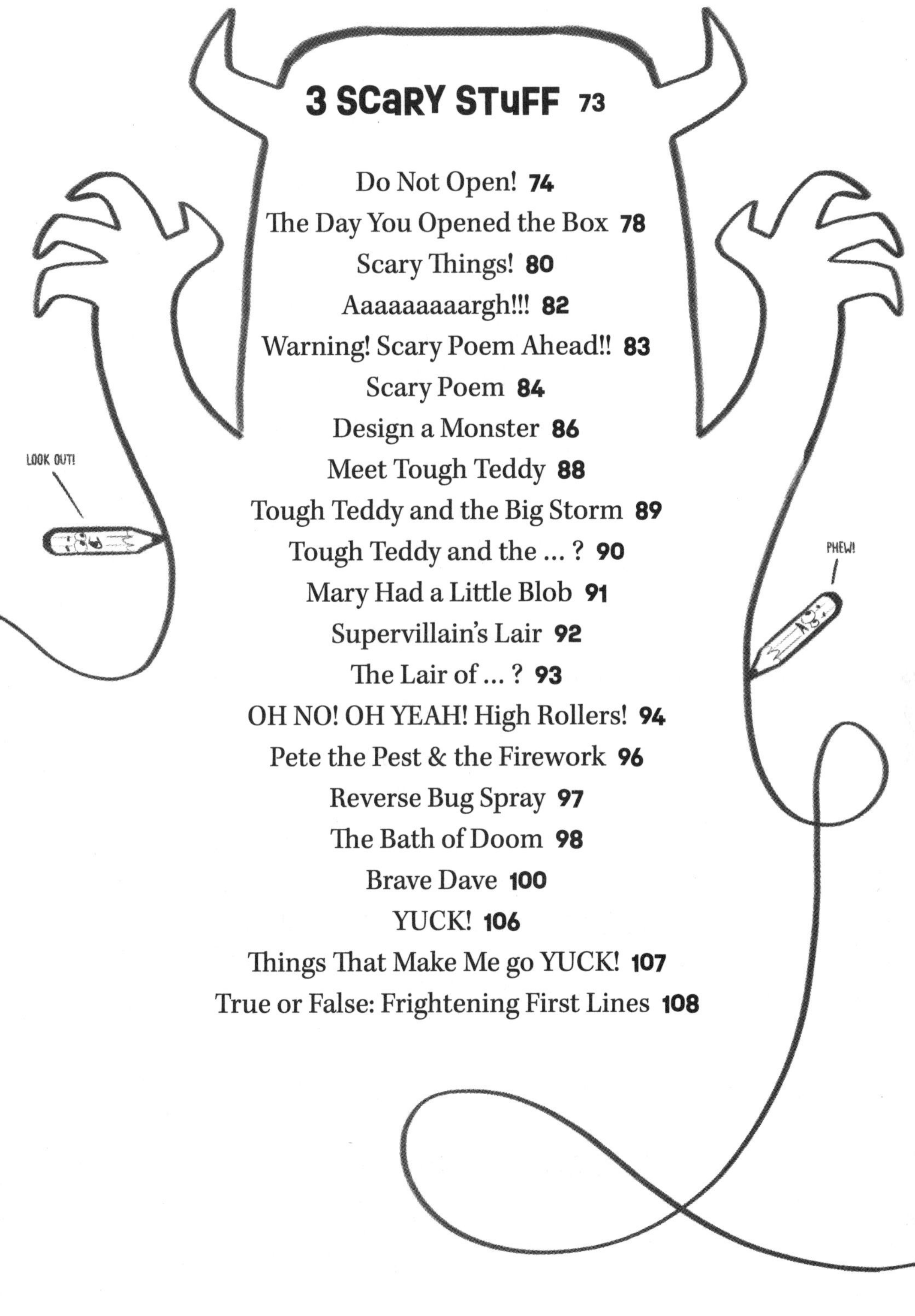

3 SCaRY STuFF 73

4 SiLLY STuFF 109

THAT WAS FUN! WHAT'S NEXT?

DUNNO, UP TO YOU I GUESS.

LET'S GO!

I LOVE reading. You can go *anywhere* in a book. *Everything* is possible and anything can happen.

I also love writing for the same reasons.

As soon as I was old enough to pick up a pencil, I wrote and drew stories to entertain, scare, surprise, annoy and (occasionally) gross out my friends and family. And I've been doing it ever since.

And now I've written this book to share some of my favourite ways to have adventures with words, pictures and ideas so that you can join in the fun.

So, what are you waiting for?

LET'S READ,
LET'S WRITE,
LET'S DRAW &

WAIT FOR ME!

1

Amazing Adventures

Hey, want to take a ride in a time machine? Want to jump down a very deep hole and discover a whole new world? Or, if you're brave, maybe you'd like to try opening one of the doors of doom. **Let's go!**

TiME MACHiNE

I've always loved stories about time travel, both reading them and writing them. Imagine travelling back to the time of the dinosaurs!

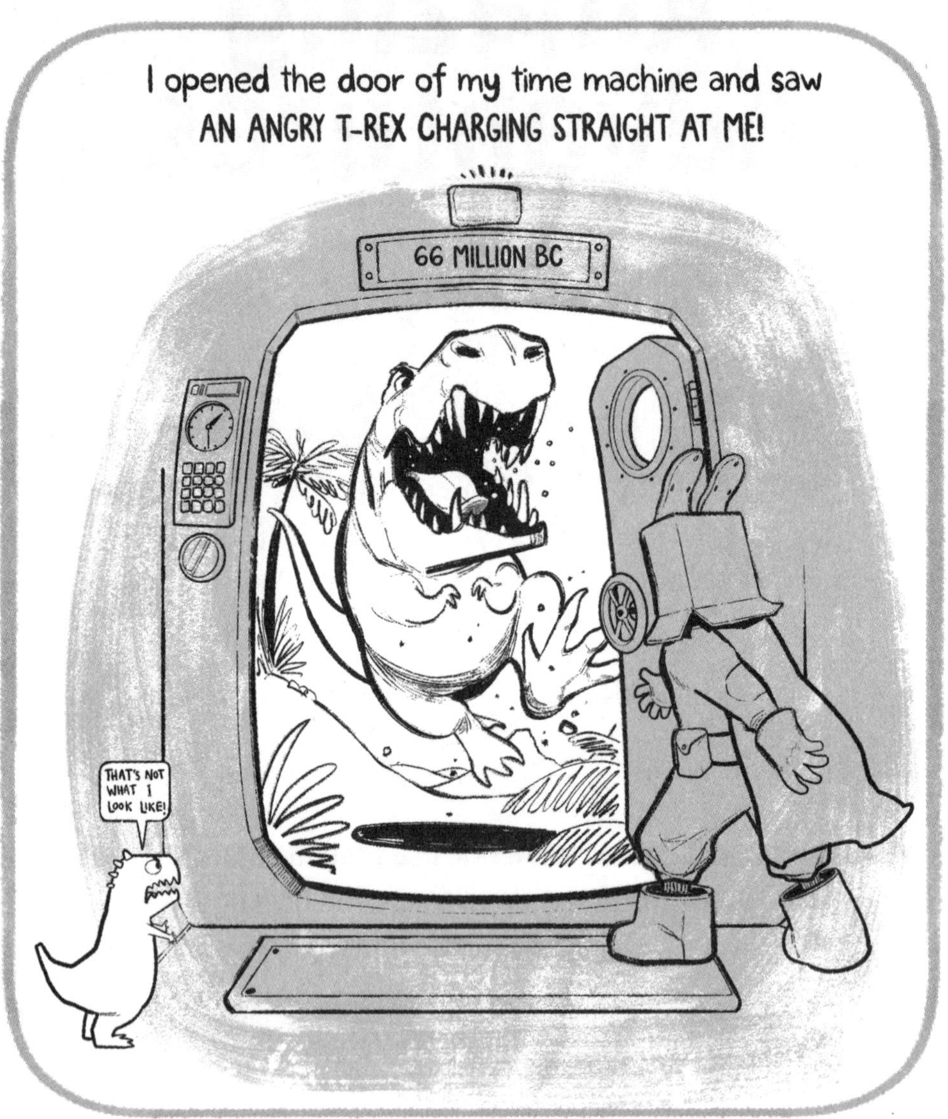

Or imagine travelling forward into the distant future.

I opened the door of my time machine and saw A ROBOT USING AN M.P.D. (MOBILE PERSON DEVICE)

2189 AD

Your time machine has just landed. **When and where are you?** Write about what you see and draw it.

I opened the door of my time machine and saw ....

....

A DaY IN THE LIFE OF a ROCK

I like to imagine what the world looks like from the point of view of other people, animals and other objects ... even a rock could have an exciting story to tell.

THE END

ADVENTURE MOBILE

Every good adventurer needs an all-terrain adventure mobile with all the features necessary to deal with any possible adventure that might come their way. Like this one ...

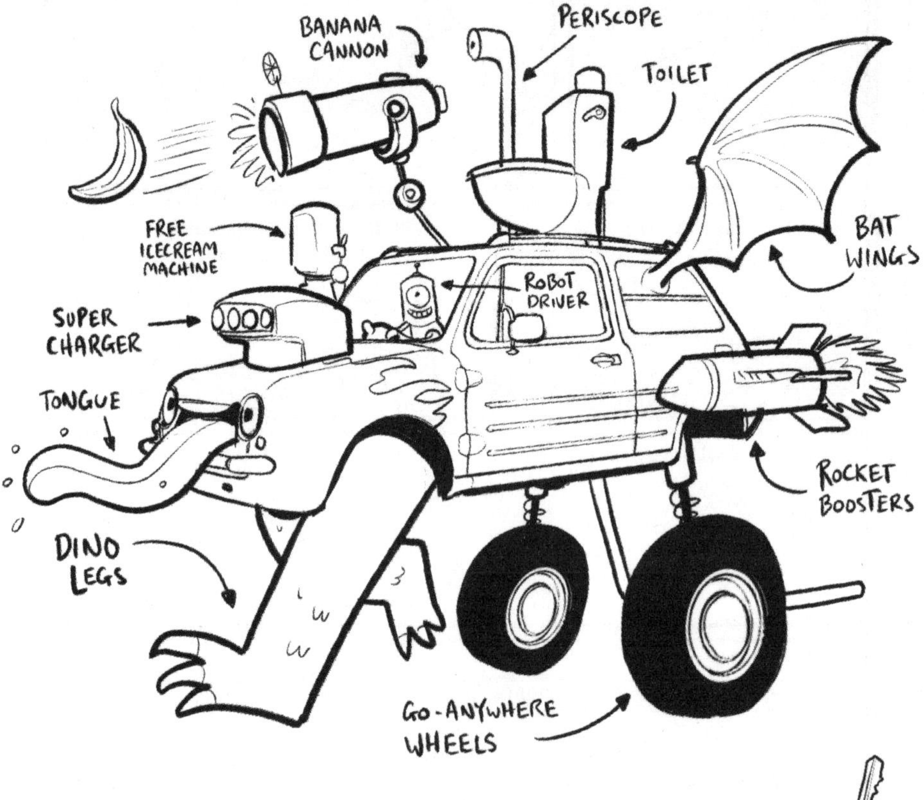

What would your ideal adventure mobile be? Remember, it's imaginary, so it can be ANYTHING and have any features you would like! Park it in the garage on the opposite page.

I WONDER WHAT KIND OF THINGS YOU MIGHT NEED ON AN ADVENTURE?
WHAT KIND OF VEHICLE WILL IT BE? A BOAT? A CAR? A PLANE? ALL THREE?
DRAW YOURS HERE!

TRaFFiC JaMMED

I AM GLAXOID 9. I AM YOUR EVIL ROBOT AUTO-PILOT.
POP
OH NO!

OH YEAH!

RETURN TO MOTHER SHIP
OH NO!

THANKS FOR RETURNING MY SHIP!
OH YEAH!

HOPE YOU DON'T MIND IF I DROP YOU OFF HERE!
PUNT
OH NO!

FUN PARK
OH YEAH!

THE END

A VeRY DeeP HoLe

Imagine you are out looking for adventure and you find a very deep hole. There's no way of knowing how deep it is or where it might lead without jumping in. **Do you jump in? OF COURSE YOU DO!**

If you jumped into a very deep hole, what land would you like—or not like—to land in? On the page opposite draw yourself falling through the hole and into the land of your dreams ... or nightmares!

I jumped into a very deep hole and landed in the Land of ______________________

____

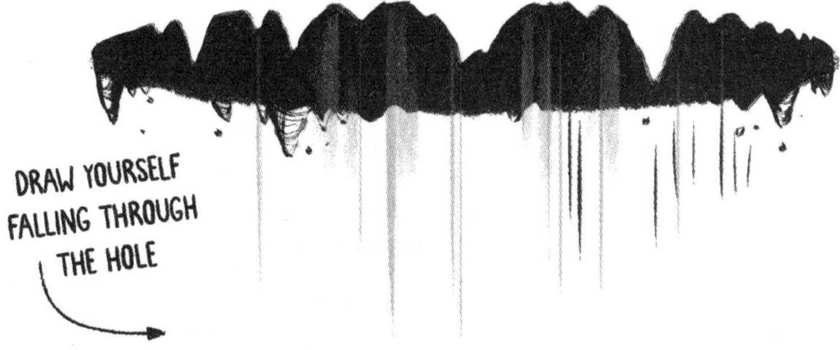

DRAW YOURSELF FALLING THROUGH THE HOLE

DRAW A PICTURE OF WHAT'S AT THE BOTTOM OF THE HOLE

DoN'T YoU HATE iT WHeN ...

Don't you hate it when you wake up bound hand and foot on a set of train tracks with a train racing towards you? It happened to me just last week. 'Oh no, not again!' I sighed. 'I'll be late for work.'

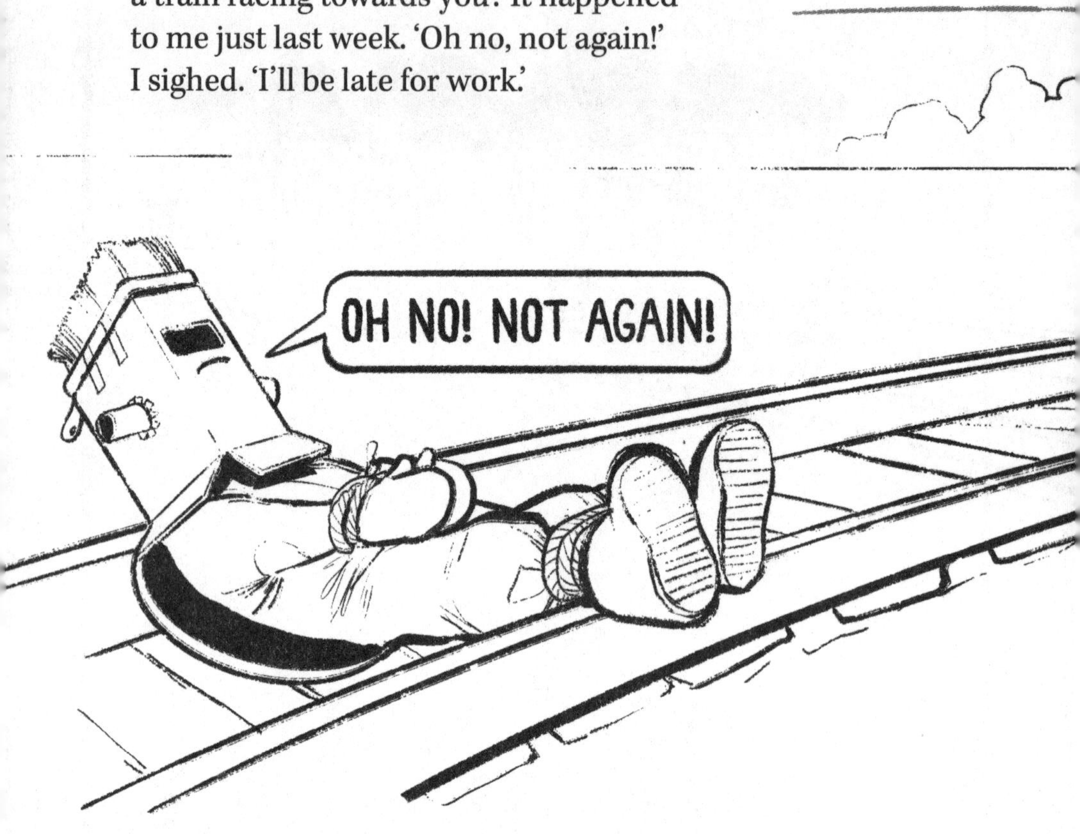

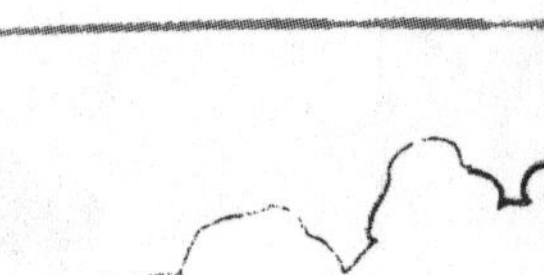

At first I wasn't overly concerned. I mean, I'm not boasting, but Harry Houdini's got nothing on me. I figured with a little flexing and some fancy breathwork I'd have those ropes snapped in a jiffy.

I took a deep breath and flexed my muscles, but, to my surprise, the ropes didn't snap.

'Well, whaddya know?' I said. 'Un-snappable rope—that's a new one!'

Fortunately, I'd spent many hours as a child developing the ability to produce laser beams from my eyes.

I stared intensely at the rope as twin beams of hot, red light shot out from my eyes. But the rope remained completely unburnt. 'Uh-oh!' I said. 'This rope is also un-laser-beamable!'

The train was only moments away.

Was this the end?

Not if I could help it.

I'd never laser-beamed a train before, but this seemed like a pretty good time to try. I turned my twin laser beams on the train and gave it all I had.

Fortunately, the train *was* laser-beamable and was vaporised instantly.

Unfortunately, the line I was tied to was quite a busy one, and I had to vaporise the 8:15, the 8:28 and the 8:52 before emergency services arrived at 9:10 and were able to cut me free, just as the 9:35 was approaching, which I jumped onto and so ended up being only a few minutes late for work. Which was lucky.

THE END

WoRST HoLIDAY eVeR

Everyone loves a good holiday, but nobody ever forgets a bad one (real or imagined). **Here's one of my worst ever!**

What's the worst holiday you've ever had, or can imagine having? Draw and label it.

My Worst Holiday Ever

DAY 1

DAY 2

DAY 3

DAY 4

DAY 5

DAY 6

TREASuRE HuNTiNG

Every good treasure hunter needs a treasure map ... and a log book to record the highs—and lows—of their treasure hunt!

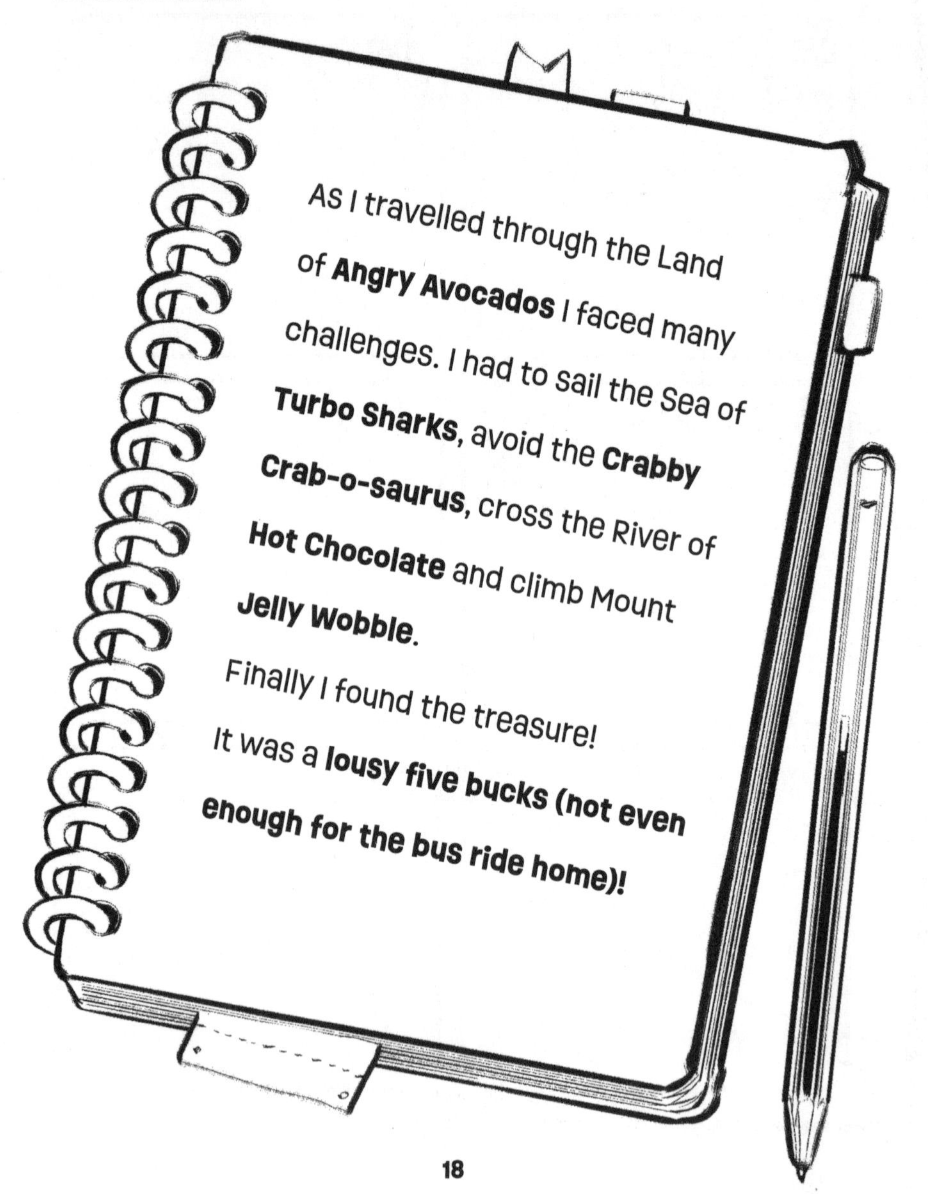

SEA OF TURBO SHARKS
MOUNT JELLY WOBBLE
CRABBY CRAB-O-SAURUS
RIVER OF HOT CHOCOLATE
MMM CHOCOLATE

MY TREaSuRE HuNT

Write about your treasure-seeking journey and mark the places you went on the map. What challenges did you face? What treasure did you find? Was it what you expected?

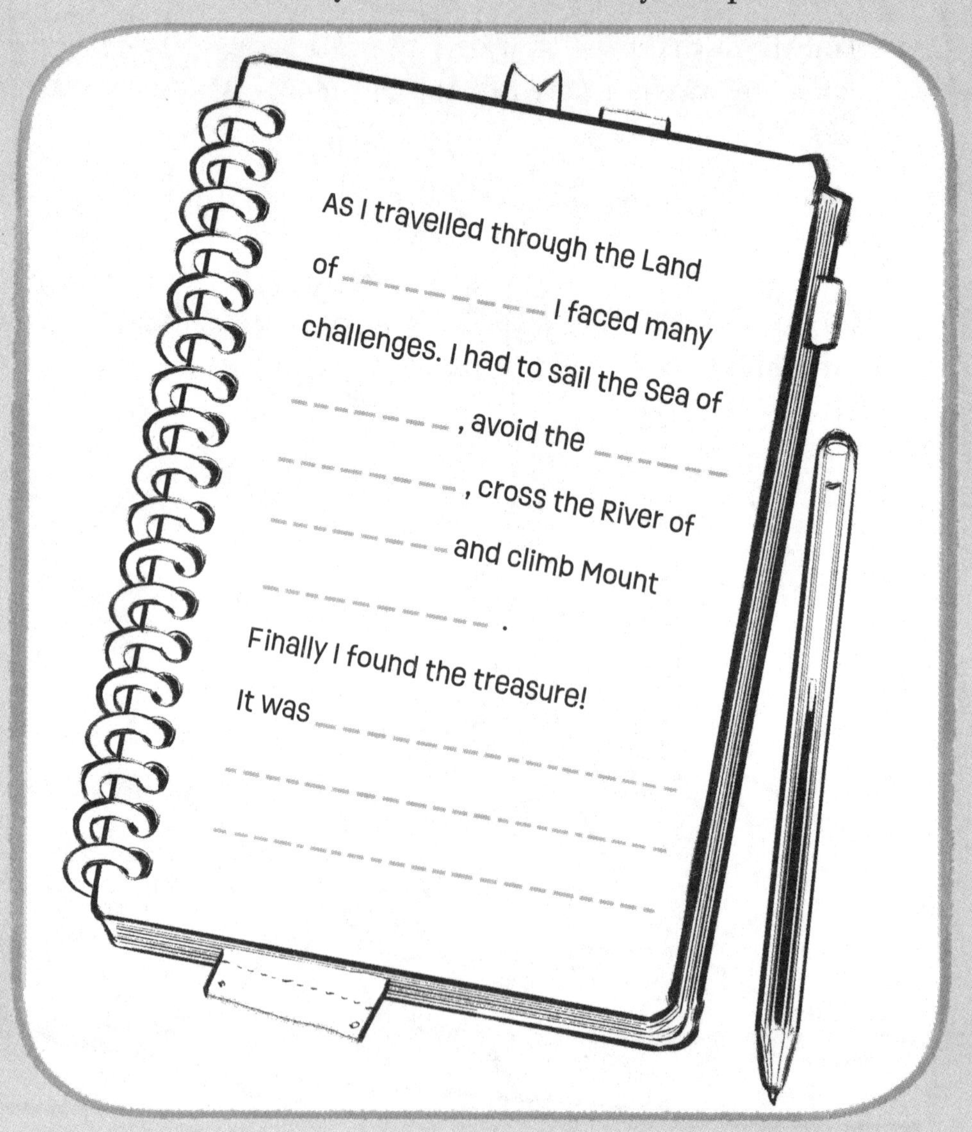

MAKE SURE YOU ADD LABELS
WHAT FEATURES CAN YOU ADD TO YOUR MAP? TREES? HILLS? ROADS? WHAT ELSE?

OH NO!
OH YEAH!

STRaNDeD

OH NO!

OH YEAH!

EVIL CRUISE
OH NO!

WEEVIL CRUISE
OH YEAH!

POP
EVIL
WEEVIL CRUISE
OH NO!

EVIL
WEEVIL CRUISE
OH YEAH!

OH NO!
OH YEAH!
OH NO!
OH YEAH!
SPLASH!
OH NO!
THE END.
OH YEAH!!

OH NO! NOT AGAIN!
I HATE IT WHEN I WAKE UP AND MY BED IS FLOATING IN THE MIDDLE OF THE OCEAN.

Q: Why did Bob fall out of the tree?

A: Because he was a fish.

Q: Why did the fly fall off the wall?

A: Because it had a piano tied to its leg.

THE DooRS oF DooM: a choose-your-own adventure

You are in a dungeon. (Don't ask me why, you just are.) There are 7 doors. One door leads to freedom. The other 6 lead to certain doom. Which one will you pick? Good luck and choose wisely!

You open Door 1.
A giant head-swallower jumps out and swallows your head. You are doomed.
THE END.

You open Door 2.
A big white box comes flying towards you. You are crushed by a refrigerator.
THE END.

You open Door 3.
You are in a room full of adorable puppies! They jump up and start licking you. But there are so many of them, you end up drowning in puppy drool.
THE END.

You open Door 4.
The door explodes.
You explode.
THE END.

You open Door 5.
It's the door to a lift.
But the lift isn't there.
You fall. You keep on
falling. Forever.
THE END.

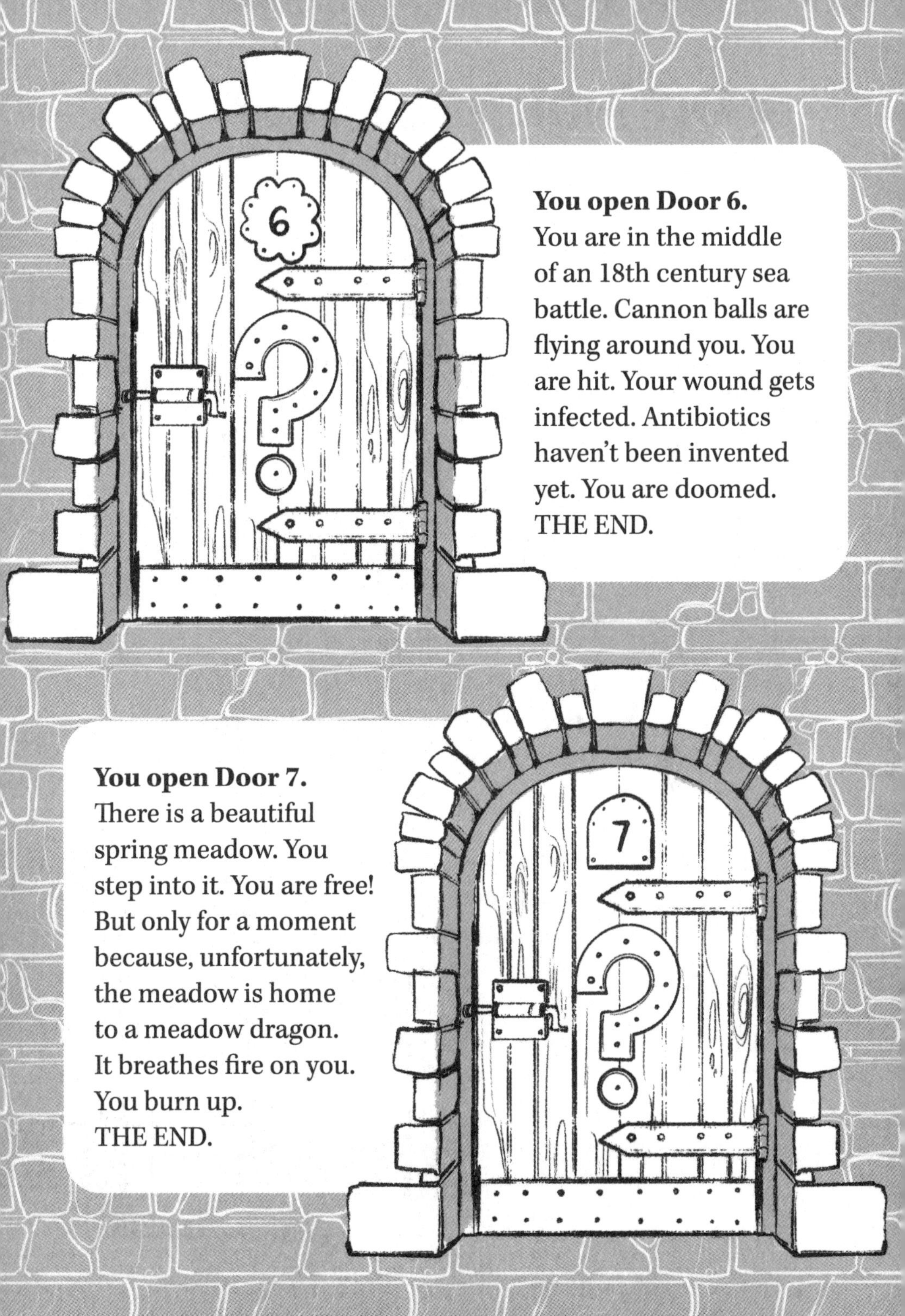

You open Door 6.
You are in the middle of an 18th century sea battle. Cannon balls are flying around you. You are hit. Your wound gets infected. Antibiotics haven't been invented yet. You are doomed. THE END.

You open Door 7.
There is a beautiful spring meadow. You step into it. You are free! But only for a moment because, unfortunately, the meadow is home to a meadow dragon. It breathes fire on you. You burn up.
THE END.

GiANT FiGHTING RoBoT MAN Q&A

Q: Can you pat a puppy?

A: Yes, I can pat a puppy. I can pat *twenty* puppies. I am GIANT FIGHTING ROBOT MAN—I can do ANYTHING!

Q: Can you bake a birthday cake?

A: Yes, I can bake a birthday cake. I can bake *fifty* birthday cakes! And I can pat twenty puppies. I am GIANT FIGHTING ROBOT MAN!

Q: Can you push over a building?

A: Yes, I can push over a building. I can push over *one hundred* buildings! And I can bake fifty birthday cakes. And I can pat twenty puppies. I am GIANT FIGHTING ROBOT MAN!

Q: Can you fight another Giant Fighting Robot Man?

A: Yes, I can fight another Giant Fighting Robot Man. I can fight a *thousand* Giant Fighting Robot Mans! And I can push over one hundred buildings! And I can bake fifty birthday cakes. And I can pat twenty puppies. I AM GIANT FIGHTING ROBOT MAN!

Q: Can you fight yourself?

A: Yes, I can fight myself. I can smash my chest—like this! I can pull my head off—like this! I can rip my brain electrodes out—like this! I can crush my power-pack—like this! Oops. I can do anything ... but maybe I should not have done that. Goodbye ... forever!

THE ADVENTURES OF

BRICKY McBRICKFACE

BRICKY AND THE CYCLOPS

HELP!

ROAR!

STUB!

OUCH!

OOPS!

YAY!

ADVENTURE JOKES

Q: What did the first loaf of bread to climb Mount Everest say when it got to the top?
A: Nothing—loaves of bread can't talk.

Q: What's the best thing about building a time machine for a school project?
A: You can take as long as you like and still get it in by the due date.

Q: What do Dora the Explorer and Chance the Rapper have in common?
A: They have the same middle name.

MY SECRET SUPERPOWER

Imagine discovering that you have a secret superpower. What is it? **What will you do with your newly found power?**

My secret superpower is ______________________

____

____

DRAW YOURS HERE!

SaLMON QUeeN

I love fictional stories but I also love non-fictional autobiographies. And don't even get me started on *fictional* non-fictional autobiographies! (At least, that's what I think *Salmon Queen* is ... imagine if it were actually true!)

My Story

IS YOUR TITLE SERIOUS OR SILLY?

IS IT YOUR REAL NAME OR A NICKNAME?

DOES IT FEATURE A HOBBY, A SPORT OR SOMETHING ELSE YOU LOVE?

IS YOUR TITLE INTRUIGING/EXCITING/FUNNY?

Imagine you are a famous something or other and you've been asked to write your life story. Write the title of your autobiography and design the front cover.

TRuE OR FaLSE: Adventure

Can you tell which of these world records are true and which are made up? Once you know the answers, why not test someone else? You could also make up some of your own and see if you can get them to believe you.

	True	False
1. The most toilet seats broken by someone's head in one minute is 46.	○	○
2. The most socks put on one foot in 30 seconds is 28.	○	○
3. The longest non-stop run was from the Earth to the moon and back again in 3.5 days.	○	○
4. The youngest person to journey to the Earth's molten core was 16 years old.	○	○
5. The fastest speed for a motorcycle ridden blindfolded is 265.33 km/h.	○	○

(Answers: 1T, 2T, 3F, 4F, 5T)

2

Animal Tales

I love writing about animals—especially unusual ones. In this section you'll meet an enormous dog, a tiny elephant, a mighty monkey, an amazing ant, a greedy bunny, truck-driving ducks and a bandy-legged groxyl. **Let's go!**

THE DOG THAT FELL APART

ONCE UPON A TIME
THERE WAS A DOG.

ONE DAY THE DOG'S
TAIL FELL OFF.

THE NEXT DAY ITS
LEGS FELL OFF.

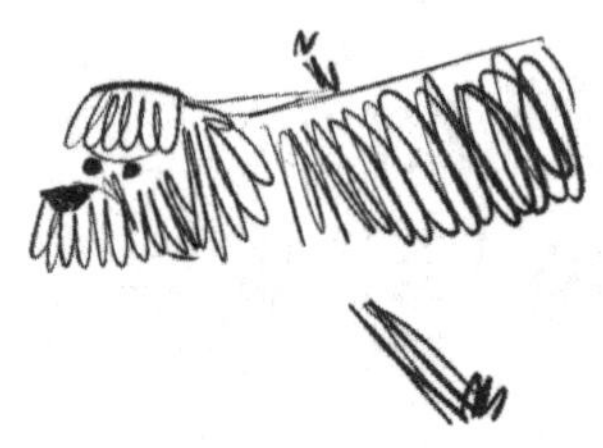

THE NEXT DAY ITS
NOSE FELL OFF.

THE NEXT DAY ITS EARS FELL OFF.

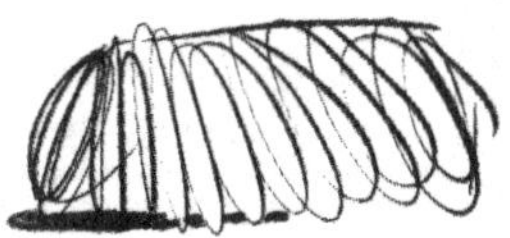

THE NEXT DAY ITS HEAD FELL OFF.

THE NEXT DAY WAS TUESDAY.

THE END.

WReSTLe-TOPIA:
Beaver Vs Egg

THIS IS HORRIFIC! BETTY IS MIXING JIMMY INTO A LIGHT FROTH!

NOW SHE'S ADDING FLOUR AND SUGAR! THE REF HAS GOT TO STEP IN HERE!
FLOUR

FOR THE FIRST TIME IN WRESTLING HISTORY ONE COMPETITOR IS ACTUALLY BAKING ANOTHER.

IN A FINAL BLOW, BETTY HAS SLICED UP JIMMY AND IS SERVING HIM TO THE CROWD.
AND I HAVE TO ADMIT, JIMMY DOES SMELL DELICIOUS!

BETTY BEAVER IS ANNOUNCED THE WINNER!

HOW DO YOU FEEL THE FIGHT WENT, JIMMY?
GEE! I REALLY THOUGHT I HAD HER IN THE FIRST ROUND BUT I GUESS IT JUST WASN'T MY DAY. FULL CREDIT TO BETTY, SHE'S ONE HECK OF A COMPETITOR!

THE END

PooKiE'S SECRET LiFE

We all know what our pets do when we're around (bark miaow, scratch, eat, sleep, poop, fight, play) but have you ever wondered **what they do when we're not there?** Write or draw or write AND draw what you think goes on.

My Pet's Secret Life

MiSSiNG PeT

Uh-oh. Looks like Pookie's lost again. **Have you seen him?**

Oh no, now your pet's lost too! Can you **make a poster** for it (or for an imaginary pet)?

MISSING!

NAME: ....

LIKES: ....

DISLIKES: ....

REWARD: ....

ANIMALS BIG AND SMALL

Big and small animals are cool, but *tiny* big animals and *gigantic* small animals are even cooler! The trick to drawing big things and small things is *comparison.* We need to see a small thing next to a big thing and a big thing next to a small thing.

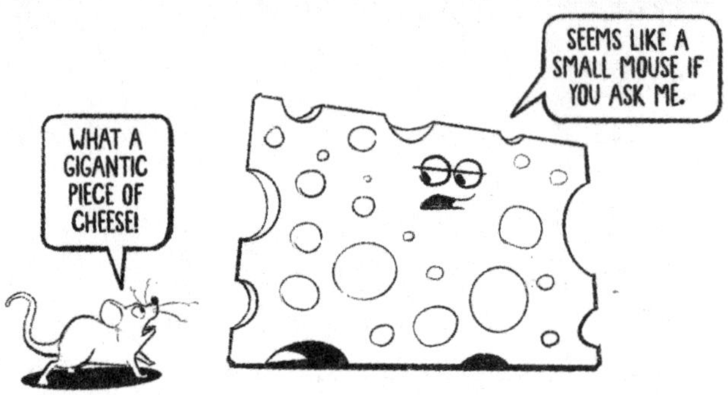

Because everything is big except the elephant in this picture we can tell that it's a small elephant!

Now, you try it. Draw a regular-sized animal in both pictures on the page opposite to see how the animal's size changes due to the size of the objects in the picture around it.

THAT'S THE SMALLEST

I'VE EVER SEEN!

DRAW YOUR SMALL THING HERE!

DRAW YOUR HUGE THING HERE!

OH MY! A GIGANTIC

IS TAKING OVER THE CITY!

 MIGHTY MONKEY

MIGHTY MONKEY IS THE STRONGEST MONKEY IN THE WORLD!

DRAW MIGHTY MONKEY CATCHING THIS FALLING SCHOOL BUS. QUICK!

DRAW MIGHTY MONKEY PUNCHING THROUGH THIS BRICK WALL.

WHAM!

DRAW MIGHTY MONKEY SWINGING THIS TIGER AROUND BY THE TAIL.

OH NO! NOT AGAIN!

I HATE IT WHEN MY DOG BECOMES ENORMOUS AND CHASES ME AROUND THE HOUSE!

PETE THE PEST
& THE SHARK TANK

-PLEASE!

PLEASE! PLEASE! PLEASE!
PLEASE! PLEASE!
PLEASE!
PLEASE!
PLEASE! PLEASE!
PLEASE! PLEASE! PLEASE!
PLEASE! PLEASE!

THE END

AUToBioGRAPHiES

An autobiography is the story of someone's (or *something's*) life written by that person (or thing). **Can you match these autobiographies with their authors?**

If you'd like to read any of these autobiographies, feel free to help the author write it in their voice!

Greedy Bunny

My bunny had been feeling a bit sick and when we had it X-rayed at the vet we could see why! It had eaten

THe aMaZING aNT

Once upon a time there was an ant. But this was no ordinary ant—this was an AMAZING ant!

And the amazing ant crawled along the ground and came to a stick. And the amazing ant crawled up the stick and the amazing ant crawled over the stick and the amazing ant crawled down the stick.

And the amazing ant crawled along the ground and came to a blade of grass. And the amazing ant crawled up the blade of grass and the amazing ant crawled over the blade of grass and the amazing ant crawled down the blade of grass.

And the amazing ant crawled to Las Vegas, won 10 million dollars and bought a red sports car.

And the amazing ant left Las Vegas and came to a stick. And the amazing ant drove up the stick and the amazing ant drove over the stick and the amazing ant drove down the stick.

THE END

Do you think Mary has learned her lesson?

Create your own Contrary Mary story to find out!

Contrary Mary

NO!

AND THE ______________________

CRiTTER PiCS

What do the names of the critters suggest to you? **Draw them.** The first one has been done for you.

SPECIMEN CARD
THE TERRIBLE BATSWITCH
NAME
SPECIMEN CARD
XORGOTON
NAME

DUCKS IN TRUCKS

There was a duck. His name was Chuck.
Chuck the Duck drove an ice-cream truck.

But one wet day Chuck's truck got stuck.

'What bad luck,' said Chuck the Duck.
'My ice-cream truck is stuck in muck.'

But then along came Chuck's friend Buck
in his brand-new, shiny, muck-sucking truck!

'Hey, Buck,' said Chuck,
'my truck is stuck. My truck
is stuck in all this muck.'

'You're in luck,' said
Buck the Duck.
'I can get your truck unstuck.
I can suck up all the muck
with the muck-sucker-upper
on my muck-sucking truck!'

'Thank you, thank you, Buck,' said Chuck.
'What are friends for?' said Buck to Chuck.
Buck's muck-sucker began to suck.
It sucked and sucked and sucked and sucked
until all the muck had been sucked up.

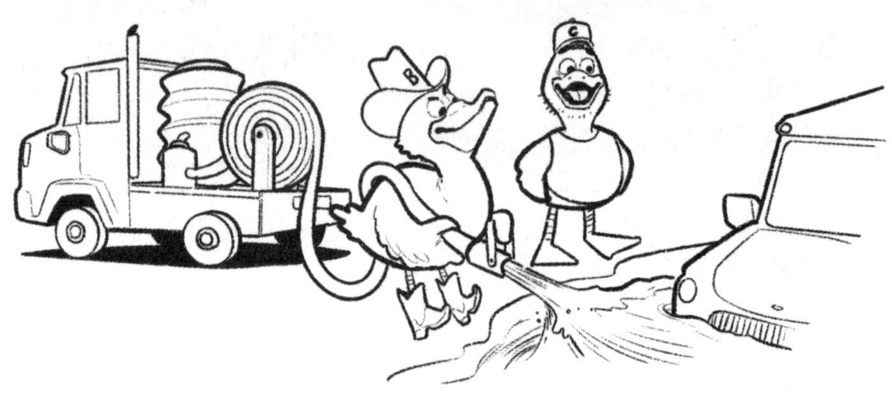

'Hooray,' cried Chuck
as he ran to his truck.

'Get back, Chuck!' yelled Buck the Duck.
'I haven't yet shut my muck-sucker up.'
But it was too late for Chuck the Duck—
he got sucked up into the truck.

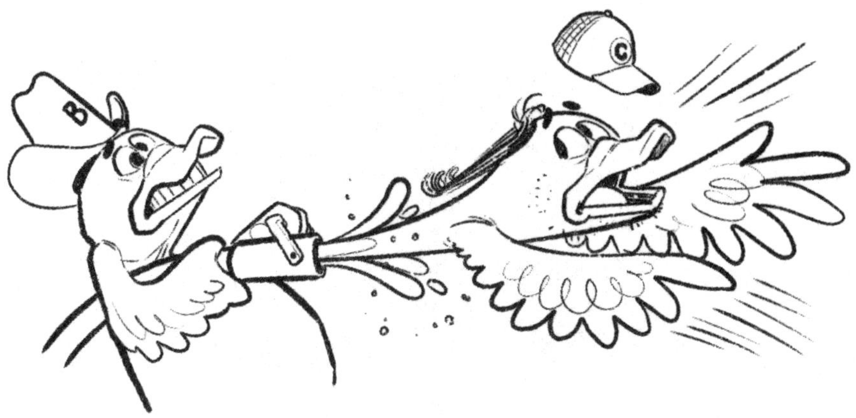

And then the muck-sucker
sucked up Buck!

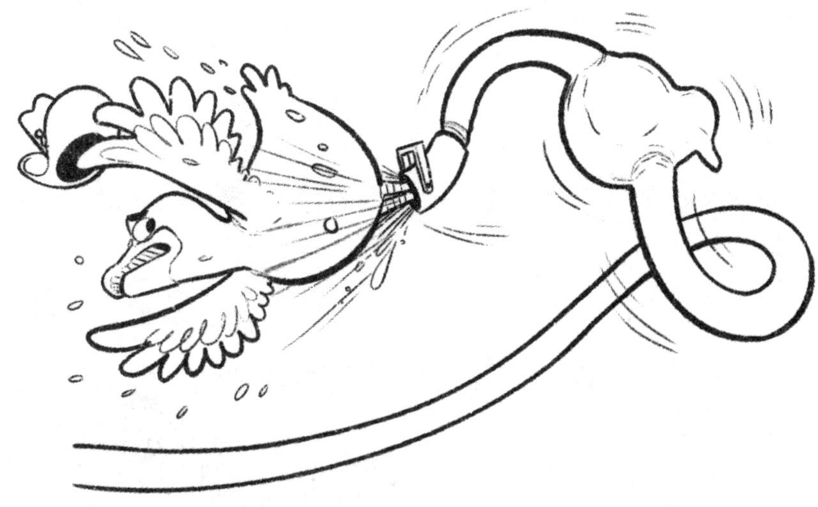

The muck-sucker-upper just kept on sucking. It sucked and sucked and sucked and sucked ... until Buck the Duck's brand-new truck got too full and it blew up!

Out flew Chuck.
Out few Buck.
Out flew all the sucked-up muck.

‘Boo hoo,’ cried Buck.
‘My brand-new truck!
My brand-new, shiny truck blew up!’

‘Don’t cry, Buck,’ said the kind duck Chuck.
‘We can share my ice-cream truck.’
‘Do you mean it, Chuck?’ said Buck.
‘What are friends for?’ said Chuck to Buck.
So Buck hopped up with Chuck the Duck
and they drove off together in their ice-cream truck.

THE END

CHeeSe QUeST

CAN YOU HELP MAX THE MOUSE GET TO THE CHEESE? DRAW HIM A FEW TIMES ACROSS EACH PAGE AS HE NAVIGATES THIS DANGEROUS KITCHEN.

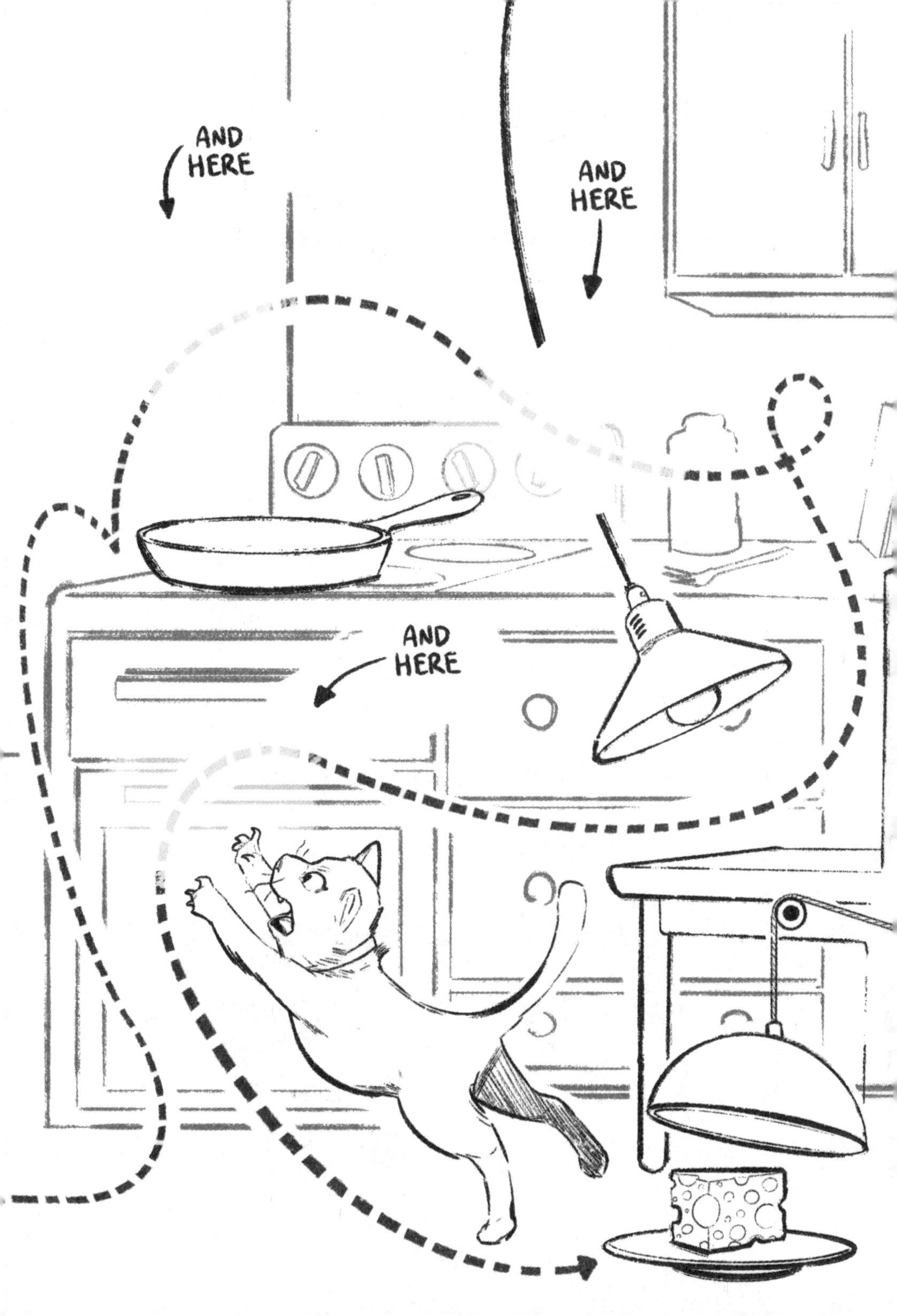
AND HERE
AND HERE
AND HERE

KoALA JoKES

Q: Why did the koala fall out of the tree?
A: Because it was dead.

Q: Why did the second koala fall out of the tree?
A: Because it was hit by the first koala.

Q: Why did the third koala fall out of the tree?
A: It thought it was a game and joined in.

Q: Why did the fourth koala fall out of the tree?
A: Accident investigators believe it was due to a combination of factors, including high winds, heavy rainfall and slippery branches.

TRuE OR FaLSE:
aNIMaL BOOKS

Can you tell which of these book titles are real and which are made up? Once you know the answers, why not test someone else? You could also make up some of your own and see if you can get your friends and family to believe you.

	True	False
1. Fish Who Answer the Telephone	○	○
2. Harnessing the Earthworm	○	○
3. Frog and Toad are Friends	○	○
4. Showbiz Tricks for Cats	○	○
5. Explosive Spiders and How to Make Them	○	○
6. Pigs I Have Known	○	○
7. The Saggy Baggy Elephant	○	○

(Answer: They are ALL actual books!)

3

Scary Stuff

I dare you to open the box that must not be opened. I dare you to read the scariest poem ever written. I dare you to design the ultimate monster. Well, what are you waiting for? You're not scared, are you? **Let's go!**

DO NOT OPeN!

Imagine you find a box that is clearly labelled **'WARNING! DO NOT OPEN!'** Should you open it? It's hard not to, because there might be something amazing in there.

But, then, there could be something really bad in there!

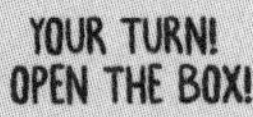
YOUR TURN!
OPEN THE BOX!

DRAW WHAT COMES OUT OF THE BOX

I opened the box and to my
HORROR out came

WARNING!
DO NOT OPEN!

DRAW WHAT COMES OUT OF THE BOX

I opened the box and to my DELIGHT out came ....

....

....

THE DAY YOU OPENED THE BOX

BE CAREFUL!

WHY? BUTTERFLIES ARE HARMLESS!

UH-OH.
NOT THESE ONES ... THEY'VE GOT FANGS.

VAMPIRE BUTTERFLIES!

RUN!

I TOLD YOU IT WAS A BAD IDEA!
THE END.

SCaRY THiNGS!

The speaker in this picture is scared of many things and they are all happening at once. Can you identify them all?

BOOOOOO!
BE FUNNIER!
YEAH! WE
HATE THIS!

Draw a picture of ALL the things you are scared of ALL happening to you—or someone else—ALL at the same time.

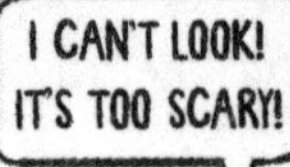

Aaaaaaaaargh!!!

***You will see the scary poem**

'Twas late one night I heard a sound—
a scratching at my door.
'Who is it?' I cried, to no reply,
so I grabbed my vorpal sword.

Sword in hand, I opened the door
and stepped into the night.
I heard a rustling behind a tree,
and steeled myself to fight.

I wheeled around
and swung my sword.
I swung with all my might!
But there was nothing there at all—
just pitch-black endless night.

And then I heard a low miaow
and saw a welcome sight:
'Mittens!' I cried. 'You naughty puss!
You gave me such a fright!'

But as I cradled Mittens,
with relief and much delight,
a horrible Jabberwock snuck up
and devoured us in one bite!

And so 'tis in the spirit world
that Mittens and I now dwell.
And I am cursed for evermore
this tragical tale to tell.

DESiGN a MONSTER

Think up the most terrifying, horrible, disgusting, vile, vicious, life-threatening monster you can. Draw its picture (if you dare!) and fill in its SCARY MONSTER I.D. badge.

SCARY
MONSTER I.D.
DRAW
YOUR
MONSTER
HERE!
NAME:
HABITAT:
STINK RATING: ___ /10

MEET TOUGH TEDDY

IF TOUGH TEDDY BREAKS HE JUST SEWS HIMSELF BACK UP.

INSTEAD OF EATING HONEY TOUGH TEDDY SAVES TIME BY JUST EATING LIVE BEES.

TOUGH TEDDY LIKES PICNICS BUT INSTEAD OF A PICNIC RUG HE USES BROKEN GLASS.

INSTEAD OF BRUSHING HIS TEETH TOUGH TEDDY EATS A TOOTHBRUSH EVERY NIGHT.

AT NIGHT TOUGH TEDDY JUST CUDDLES A CHAINSAW.

WHEN TOUGH TEDDY SLEEPS HE SAYS GRRRR! INSTEAD OF ZZZZZ.

TOUGH TEDDY

AND THE BIG STORM

ONE NIGHT TOUGH TEDDY WAS GETTING READY FOR BED.

HE HAD A NICE WARM MUG OF CHILLI SAUCE AND A BOOK ABOUT EXPLOSIONS TO GET HIM TO SLEEP.

HE WAS JUST NODDING OFF WHEN HE HEARD A LOUD CLAP OF THUNDER.

TOUGH TEDDY GROWLED A WARNING THEN WENT OUTSIDE.

IN ONE GREAT LEAP TOUGH TEDDY JUMPED UP AND SLAPPED THE STORM CLOUD SO HARD IT RAINED ITSELF.

THE CLOUD QUICKLY DRIFTED AWAY AND TOUGH TEDDY FELL FAST ASLEEP.

CREATE YOUR OWN TOUGH TEDDY STORY

TOUGH TEDDY

AND THE ____________________

MaRY HaD a LiTTLE BLoB

Mary had a little blob,
A blobby little thing,
That blobbed along behind her
On a knotty piece of string.

It blobbed along to school one day.
(Despite the no-blobs rule!)
It made the children cry and scream
To see that blob at school.

SUPERVILLAIN'S LAIR

Every supervillain needs a lair, whether it be a high-tech underground base, a spooky castle or a lavish mansion. Design a lair for a supervillain. Don't forget to label all its special features.

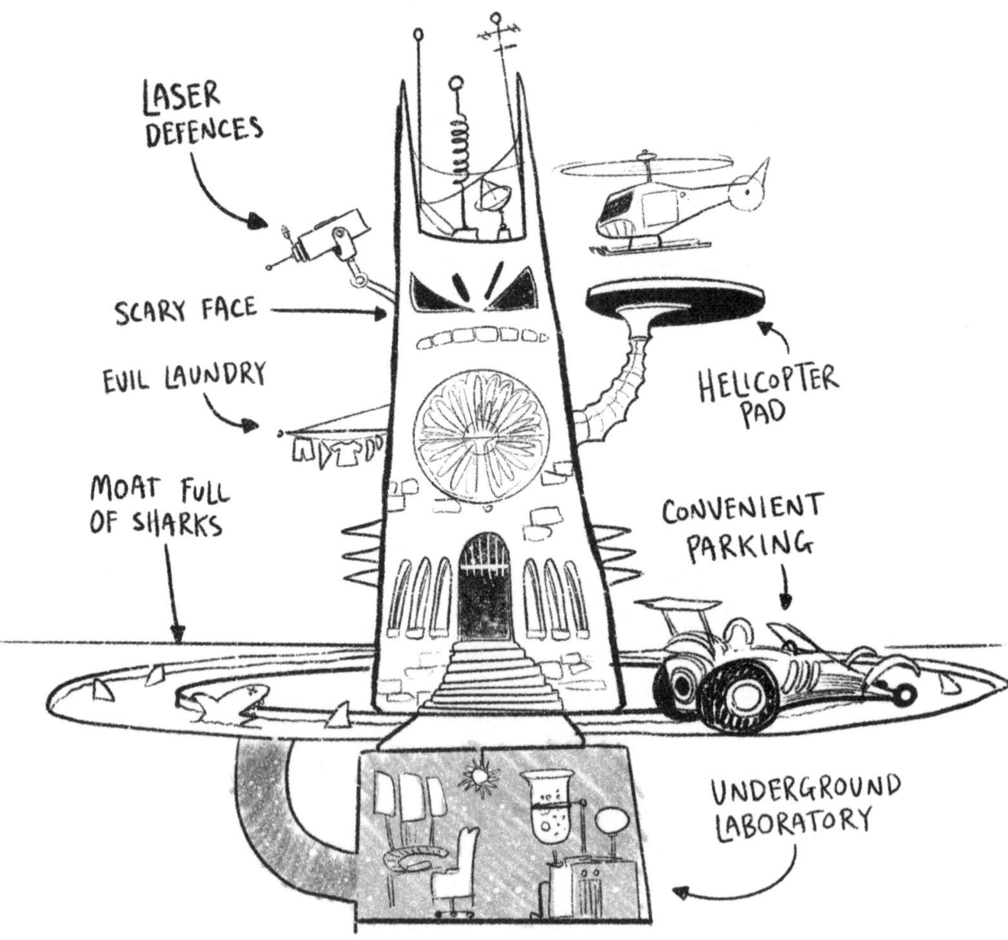

THE LAIR OF ______________

PUT THE NAME OF YOUR VILLAIN HERE!

MAKE SURE TO LABEL THE FEATURES OF THE LAIR!

ARE THERE ANY SHARKS IN THERE? THERE'S GOT TO BE SHARKS IN THERE!

HiGH ROLLeRS!

GOTCHA!
OH NO!

YOU MUST BE THIS SHORT TO RIDE THE ROLLER-COASTER
OH YEAH!

OH NO!

OH YEAH!

OH NO!

OH YEAH!
$
THE END

PETE THE PEST
& THE FIREWORK

PLEASE! PLEASE! PLEASE!
PLEASE! PLEASE!
PLEASE! PLEASE!
PLEASE! PLEASE! PLEASE!
PLEASE! PLEASE! PLEASE!
PLEASE! PLEASE!

THE END

OH NO! NOT AGAIN!
BIG BUG
I HATE IT WHEN I ACCIDENTALLY BUY REVERSE BUG SPRAY THAT MAKES THE BUGS BIGGER!

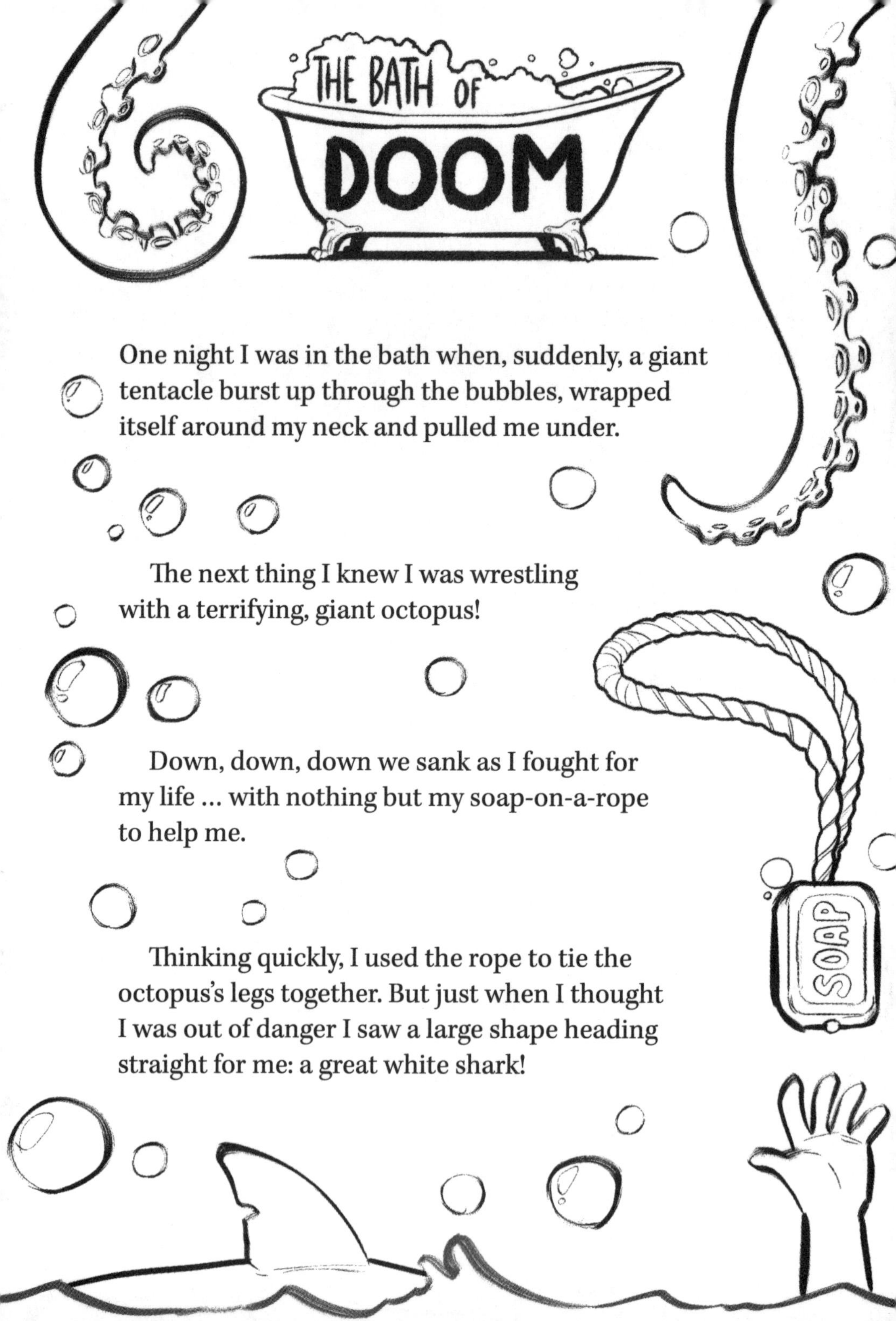

THE BATH OF DOOM

One night I was in the bath when, suddenly, a giant tentacle burst up through the bubbles, wrapped itself around my neck and pulled me under.

The next thing I knew I was wrestling with a terrifying, giant octopus!

Down, down, down we sank as I fought for my life … with nothing but my soap-on-a-rope to help me.

Thinking quickly, I used the rope to tie the octopus's legs together. But just when I thought I was out of danger I saw a large shape heading straight for me: a great white shark!

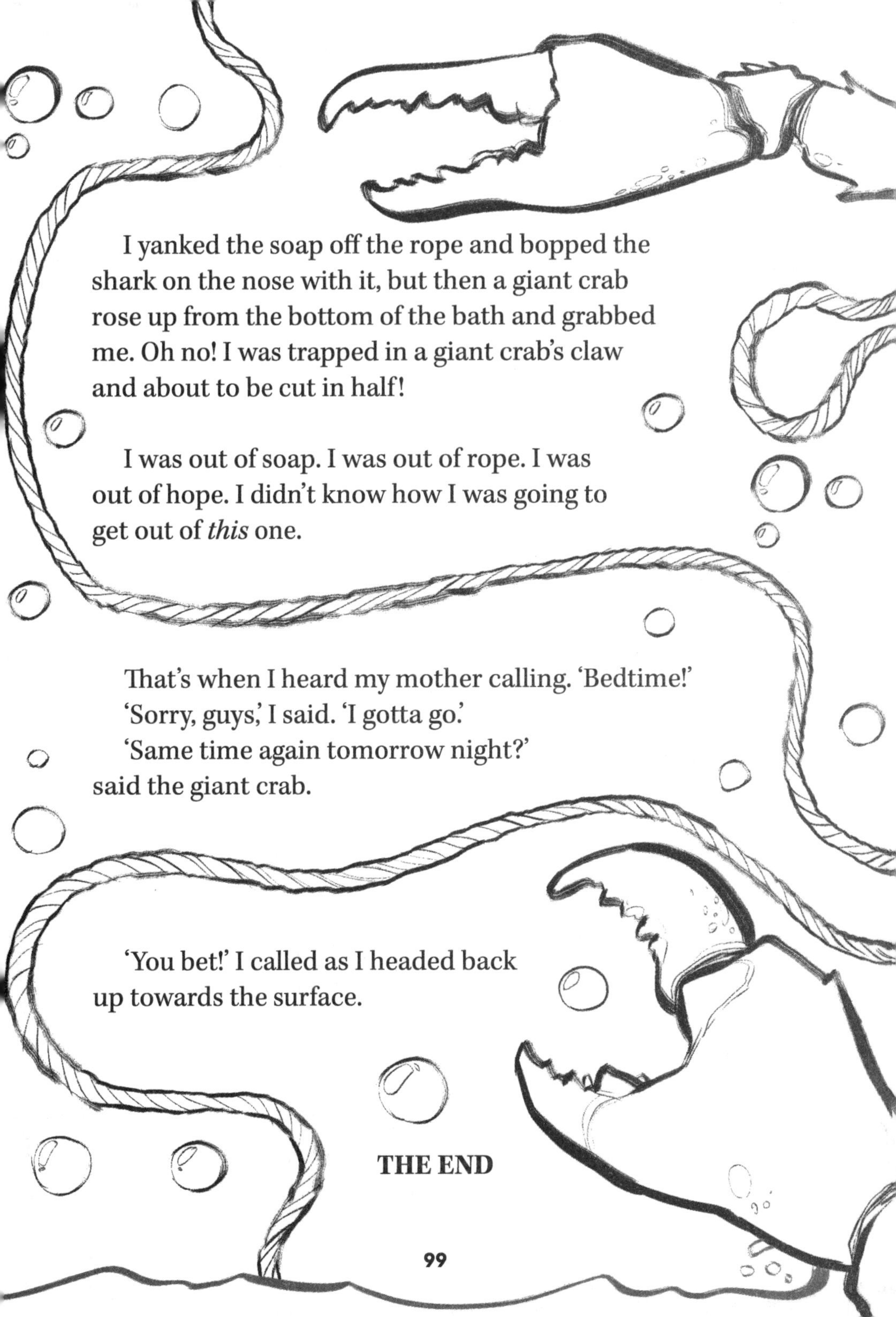

I yanked the soap off the rope and bopped the shark on the nose with it, but then a giant crab rose up from the bottom of the bath and grabbed me. Oh no! I was trapped in a giant crab's claw and about to be cut in half!

I was out of soap. I was out of rope. I was out of hope. I didn't know how I was going to get out of *this* one.

That's when I heard my mother calling. 'Bedtime!'

'Sorry, guys,' I said. 'I gotta go.'

'Same time again tomorrow night?' said the giant crab.

'You bet!' I called as I headed back up towards the surface.

THE END

BRaVE DaVE

This is Dave,
who, during
the day, is

REALLY

REALLY

REALLY

BRAVE!

But, during the night,
when there's no light,
Dave is **NOT** brave.
He takes fright.

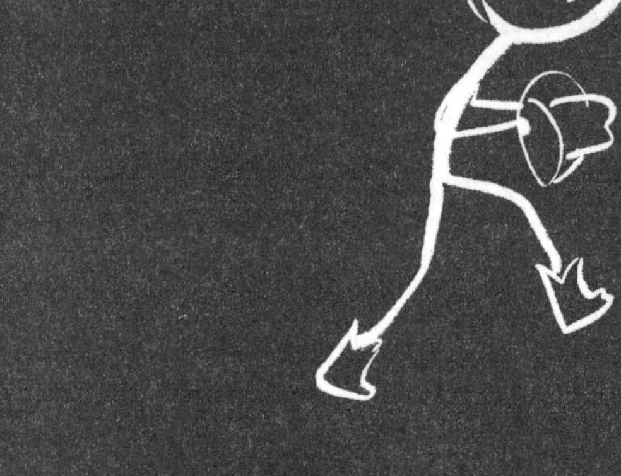

Each noise
he hears
increases
his fears.

Every
BUMP,

Every
THUMP

makes his
poor heart

JUMP!

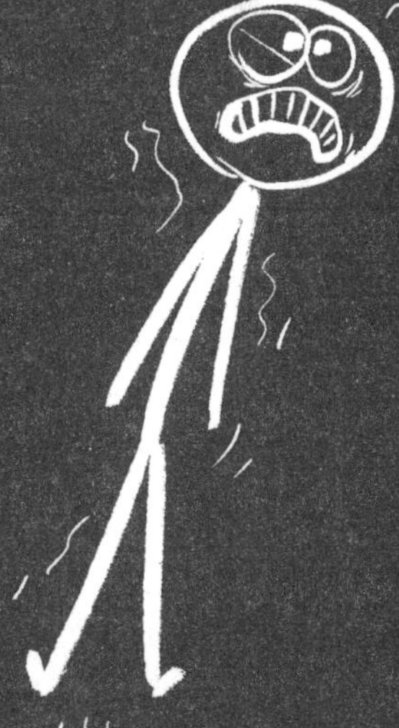

So if you need
a brave job done,
call Dave in the day ...

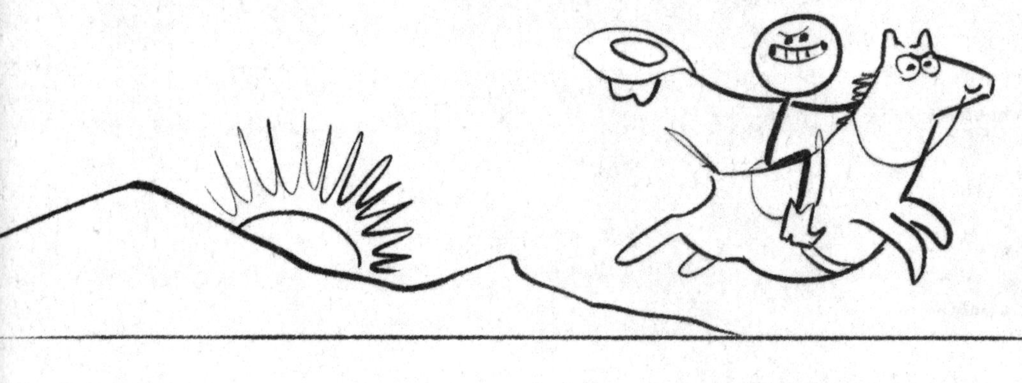

But, at night, call his mum!

THE END

YuCK!

It's a fine line between things that make you go 'EEK!' and things that make you go 'YUCK!' So let's cross it ...

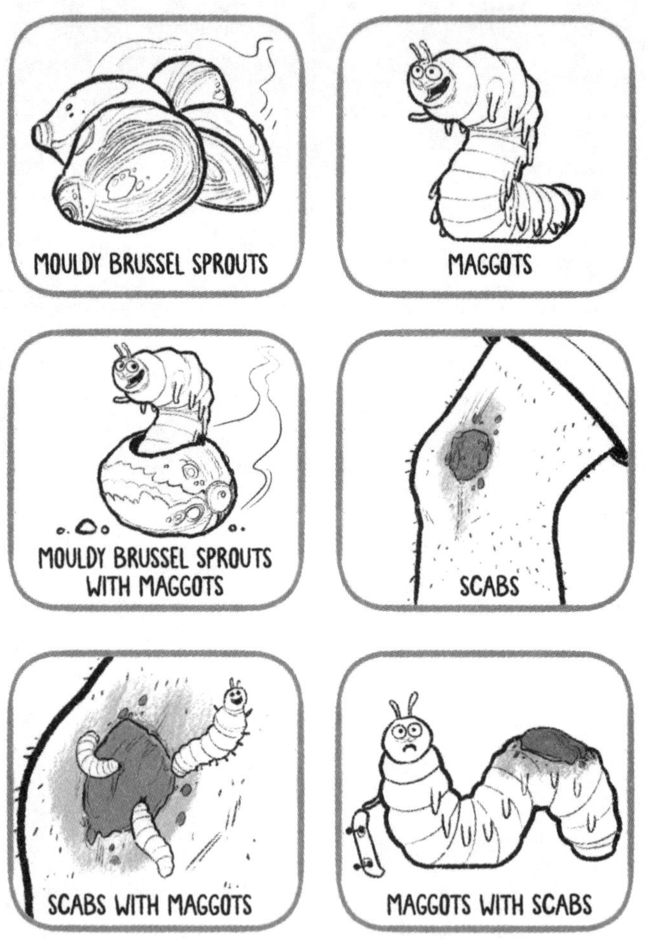

What makes you go 'YUCK!'? Create an illustrated list and show it to someone else to see if it makes them go 'YUCK' too.

Things that make ME go YUCK!

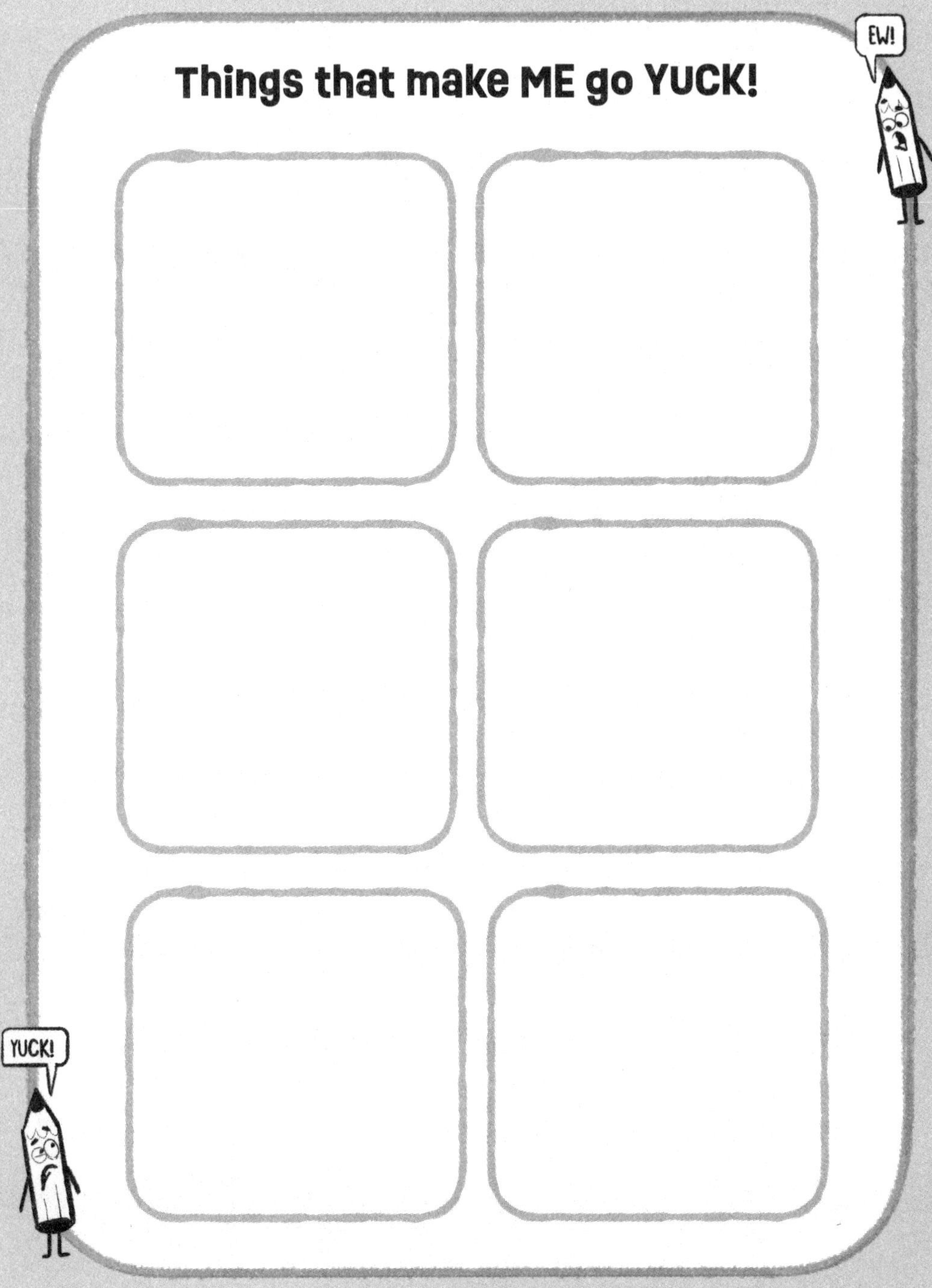

TRuE OR FaLSE: FRiGHTENING FiRST LiNES

Can you tell which of these first lines from books are true and which are made up? Once you know the answers, why not test someone else? You could also make up some of your own and see if you can get them to believe you.

	True	False
1. Marley was dead, to begin with.	○	○
2. No, your cat won't eat your eyeballs. Not right away, at least.	○	○
3. Kidnapping children is never a good idea. All the same, sometimes it has to be done.	○	○
4. It was a dark and stormy night.	○	○
5. 'My lunchbox is trying to eat me!' I screamed, but there was nobody left alive to hear.	○	○
6. It was a very fine day, until something tried to eat him.	○	○

Answers: 1. True: A Christmas Carol 2. True: Will My Cat Eat My Eyeballs? 3. True: Monster Mission 4.True: A Wrinkle in Time 5. False: But if it were true it would be called Lunchbox of Doom. Feel free to write it. 6. True: Impossible Creatures

4

Silly Stuff

Have you ever wondered what it might be like to climb inside a microwave oven? Have you ever wanted to read a story where nothing at all happens? Or perhaps you've wished you could paint the silliest painting in the world. Well, **let's go!**

Now it's your turn. **What does that pest Pete want now?** Hint: get him to ask for something YOU'VE always wanted to do.

PETE THE PEST & THE -PLEASE!

MUM, CAN I

PLEASE! PLEASE! PLEASE!
PLEASE! PLEASE!
PLEASE! PLEASE!
PLEASE! PLEASE!
PLEASE! PLEASE! PLEASE!
PLEASE! PLEASE!

THE END.

ED aND TED (aND TED'S DoG FReD)

There was a man whose name was Ed. He lived in a shed with his friend Ted (who had a dog whose name was Fred).

Ed liked Ted.
And Ted liked Ed.
And Fred liked Ted
(but he didn't like
Ed).

One morning Fred jumped on Ed's bed. Ed said, 'Fred, get off my bed!' But Fred just growled and bit Ed's head.

Ed saw red and then he said,
'I'm fed up with Fred always biting my head!
I'm leaving this shed!'

Ed went to his car
(which was red).
He jumped in and
away he fled.

Ted said, 'Ed!
Come back to
the shed!'
But Ed just
shook his head
and sped.

So Ted jumped in his car (which was also red).
But it wouldn't start. The battery was dead.
'Bother! Bother! Bother!' said Ted.
'I'll have to take the sled instead.'

Ted hitched up Fred to
the front of the sled,
cracked his whip and
away they sped.

Ted and Fred sped after Ed.
Ted saw Ed's red car up ahead.
'Faster, faster, Fred!' yelled Ted.

Ted and Fred were gaining on Ed, but all of a sudden Ed stopped dead.

There was a sign and that sign read:

Ted yelled, ‘Fred! Stop the sled!’
But Fred could not. On they sped!
Ted and Fred smashed into Ed!

Over the cliff Ed
plumm-et-ed
(closely
followed by Ted
and Fred).

They hit the water and sank like lead. Poor Ed and Ted and Ted's dog Fred. They were drowning and almost dead ...

when they were swallowed by a whale (called Ned) ...

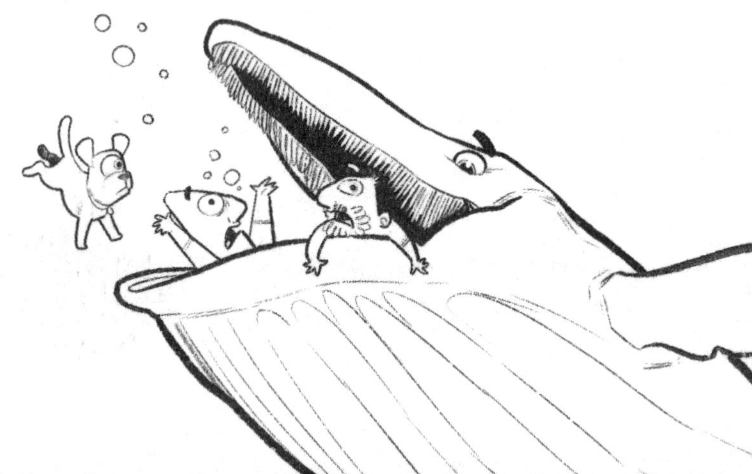

who blew them all out through the hole in his head!

Up, up, up, flew Ed and Ted.

Up, up, up flew Ted's dog Fred.

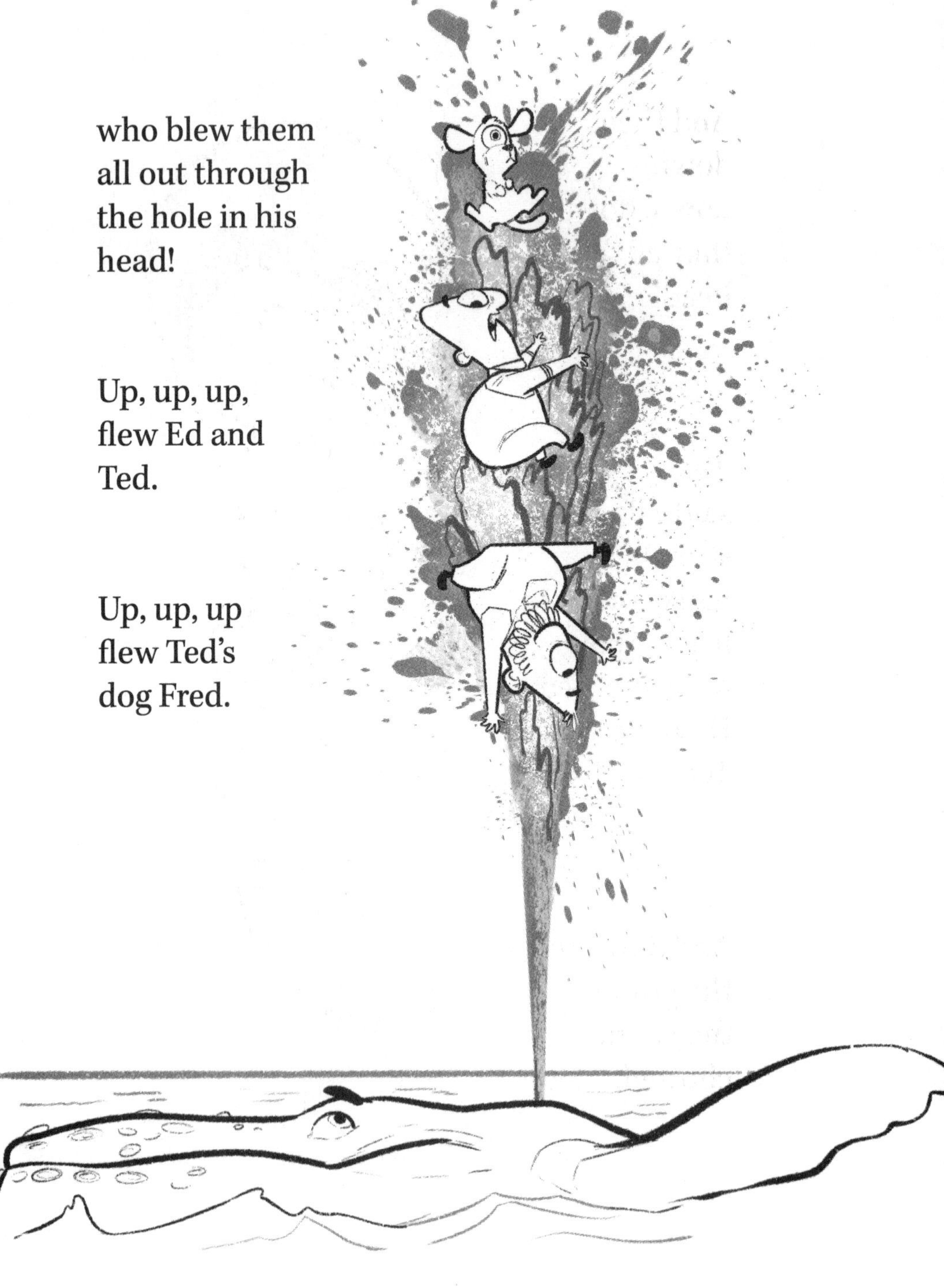

And then
down,
down, down,
they all did
head!

'Fear not!'
said Ed,
stretching a
hanky over his
head. 'Hang
on to me, Ted!
Hang on to
Ted, Fred!'

And down to
the ground
they para-
chut-ed.

‘Thank you, thank you, Ed,’ said Ted. ‘Thanks to you we are not dead.’

‘Woof! Woof! Woof!’ said Ted’s dog Fred and he jumped up and licked Ed’s head.

Ed
hugged
Fred!

Fred
hugged
Ed!

Ted
hugged
Fred!

Fred
hugged
Ted!

Ed
hugged
Ted!

Ted
hugged
Ed!

And they lived
happily ever after
(in their shed).

THE E(N)D

SiNGLe-SoUND RHYMeS

I like writing rhyming stories using only one rhyming sound (like Ed and Ted, for example). List all the words you can think of that rhyme with the words below.

Choose one group of your rhyming words and write a short poem or story using as many of them as you can.

DRAW YOUR OWN KNUCKLEHEAD HAND

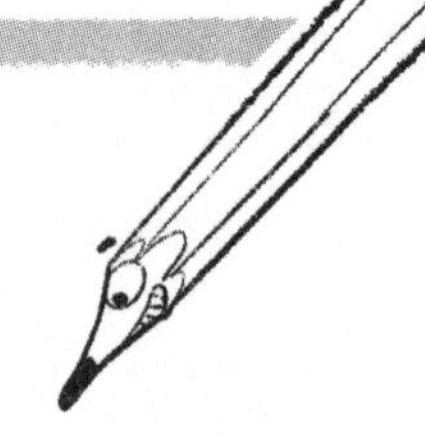

STOP BEING SO RUDE!
I DIDN'T DO ANYTHING!
TRY DRAWING YOUR OWN **KNUCKLEHEAD** ON THIS HAND
ASK AN ADULT AND THEY MIGHT LET YOU DRAW A KNUCKLEHEAD ON YOUR OWN HAND
HEY! STOP COPYING US!

SiLLY SUZY'S PAiNTiNG

What hat was Silly Suzy wearing and what did she paint?
Fill in the blanks—the pictures and the words.

Because Suzy had worn her lucky hat, she had finally painted the SILLIEST painting in the whole world.
She called it ____________________

____

Contrary Mary

AND THE 10-TONNE WEIGHT

WoRD PiCTURES

These words are drawn so that they look like what they mean. Can you draw the words on the opposite page so they describe their meaning?

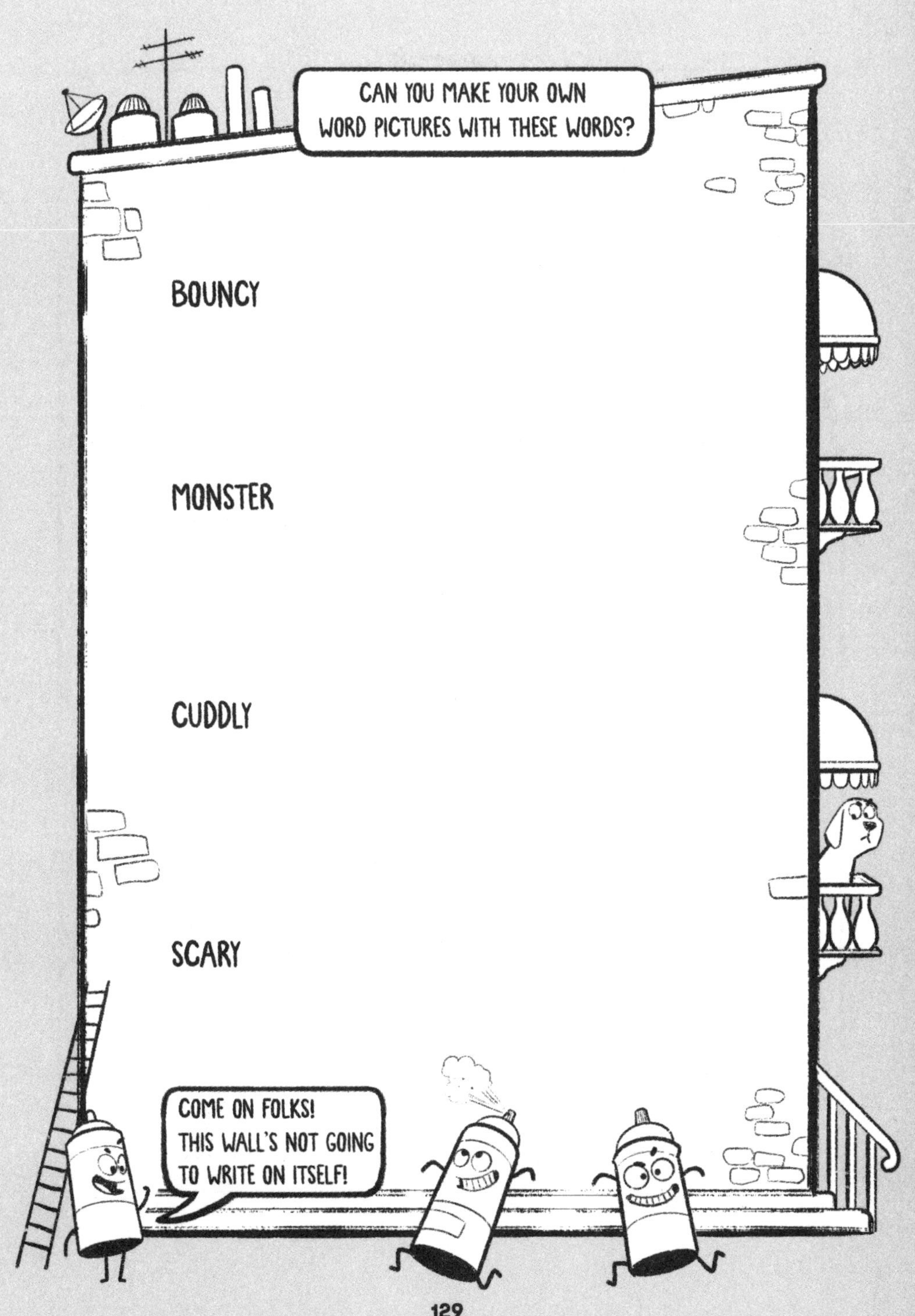
CAN YOU MAKE YOUR OWN
WORD PICTURES WITH THESE WORDS?
BOUNCY
MONSTER
CUDDLY
SCARY
COME ON FOLKS!
THIS WALL'S NOT GOING
TO WRITE ON ITSELF!

I HATE IT WHEN I'M THROWING THE BALL FOR THE DOG AND I GET CONFUSED AND END UP THROWING THE DOG INSTEAD OF THE BALL.

BoNKLE BoNKLE RiBBLE GLoP

Bonkle, bonkle, ribble glop,
Hoo ee wubble wheep yum plop!
Ap abub yah blurb su jy,
Spike vim blinkle winkle bly.
Bonkle, bonkle, ribble glop,
Hoo ee wubble wheep yum plop!

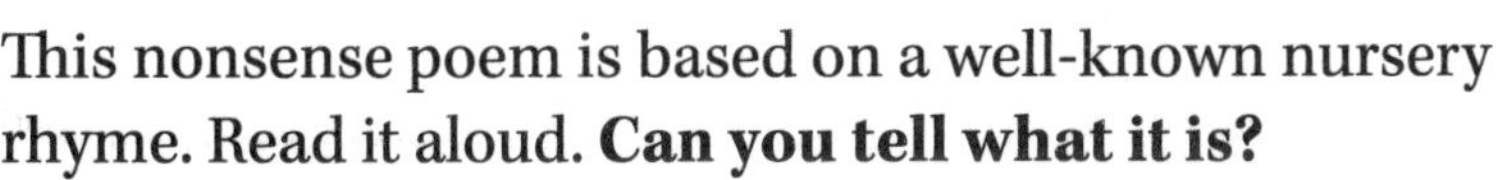

This nonsense poem is based on a well-known nursery rhyme. Read it aloud. **Can you tell what it is?**

Answer: Twinkle, twinkle, Little Star

TRuE OR FaLSE: SiLLY STaTEMENTS

Can you tell which of these statements are true and which are made up? Once you know the answers, why not test someone else? You could also make up some of your own and see if you can get them to believe you.

	True	False
1. A baby born during a flight is given free air travel for the rest of their life by the airline.	○	○
2. A cockroach can live for up to nine days without its head.	○	○
3. If you dropped a pea from the top of a skyscraper it could kill a pedestrian walking on the street below.	○	○
4. You can't sneeze with your eyes open, and if you could your eyes would pop out of their sockets.	○	○
5. Peanuts are a key ingredient in dynamite.	○	○

(Answers: 1F, 2T, 3F, 4F, 5T)

THe DAY NOTHiNG HAPPeNeD

One day
nothing
happened.

Nobody slipped on a banana skin and went skidding through the street making a complete and utter fool of themselves.

Nobody's cat turned into a dragon and took them for a wild ride through the sky.

Nobody's dog
became enormous
and chased them
around the house.

There were no
hurricanes.

There were no
earthquakes.

There were no (unnecessarily loud) burps.

It was a pretty quiet day, well, except for one tiny invasion of killer cornflakes from outer space …

but they were quickly neutralised with milk and eaten before the end of the day, with no more harm done than a slightly higher than usual number of people complaining of stomach ache.

So apart from that, nothing happened that day. Nothing happened at all.

THE END

HoW To WAVe GoODBYe iN 6 eASY STePS

SEE YA!

PLEASE!

AREN'T YOU GOING TO WAVE GOODBYE, MARY?

NO!

I'M OUTTA HERE!

ME TOO!

ANDY'S WRITING TIPS

READ AS MUCH AND AS OFTEN AS YOU CAN. FILL YOUR HEAD WITH STORIES, SONGS, POEMS, CARTOONS AND COMIC STRIPS. THE MORE IDEAS YOU PUT IN, THE MORE IDEAS WILL COME OUT.

IDEAS ARE ALL AROUND YOU. PAY ATTENTION!

WRITING IS A MUSCLE. THE MORE OFTEN YOU WRITE, THE BETTER YOU'LL GET.

COLLECT YOUR OBSERVATIONS, MEMORIES AND IDEAS IN A WRITER'S NOTEBOOK.

IF YOU'RE NOT LIKING A BOOK, STOP READING IT AND TRY ANOTHER ONE!

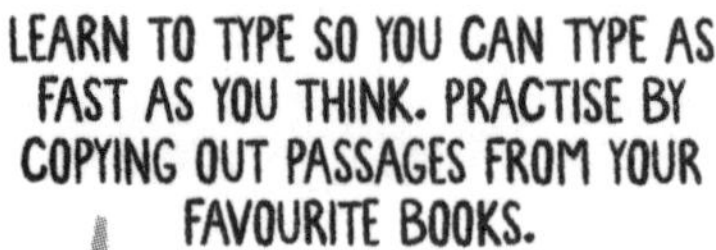

LEARN TO TYPE SO YOU CAN TYPE AS FAST AS YOU THINK. PRACTISE BY COPYING OUT PASSAGES FROM YOUR FAVOURITE BOOKS.

DON'T WORRY ABOUT GETTING PUBLISHED OR TRYING TO WRITE THE BEST STORY IN THE WORLD. JUST ENJOY THE PROCESS OF WRITING TO ENTERTAIN YOURSELF, YOUR FRIENDS OR YOUR FAMILY.

IF YOU'RE WRITING A STORY AND YOU GET STUCK, TRY MAPPING YOUR PLOT OUT AS A SERIES OF PROBLEMS AND SOLUTIONS AS DEMONSTRATED IN THE OH NO! (PROBLEM) OH YEAH! (SOLUTION) STORIES IN THIS BOOK.

IF YOU CAN, LEAVE YOUR PIECE OF WRITING FOR A WHILE BEFORE REVISING. IT'S EASIER TO EDIT ONCE YOU'VE HAD A BREAK FROM IT.

BILL'S DRAWING TIPS

MOST OF THE WORK OF DRAWING CAN BE DONE WITH THE MOST BASIC TOOLS. JUST GET STARTED WITH WHATEVER YOU HAVE ON HAND AND YOU CAN FIGURE OUT THE REST AS YOU GO.

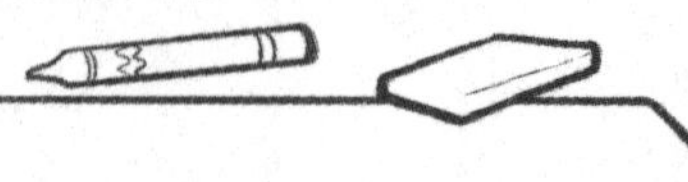

TRY NOT TO BE AFRAID OF THE GREAT WHITE EXPANSE OF A BLANK PAGE

JUST GET SOMETHING DOWN BEFORE YOU WORRY ABOUT GETTING SOMETHING GOOD DOWN.

FUN COMES FIRST!
LEARNING TECHNICAL SKILLS IS GREAT...

BUT ONLY AS A WAY TO ACCESS
BIGGER, BETTER, MORE CREATIVE KINDS OF FUN!

SPEND TIME WITH THE PICTURES YOU LIKE, YOU WANT TO ABSORB THEM LIKE YOU ARE IN A BIG POT OF STEW.

LOOK AT ALL DIFFERENT KINDS OF ART.

EVEN IF IT'S NOT THE KIND OF THING YOU WANT TO MAKE, IT WILL STILL MAKE YOUR THING BETTER!

DRAWING IS A KIND OF
COMMUNICATING
SO IT'S GOOD TO SHARE YOUR
WORK WITH OTHERS.
EVEN IF THAT'S
JUST ON THE
FAMILY FRIDGE.
DRAWING WELL IS GREAT BUT HAVING
AN ACTIVE IMAGINATION IS PERHAPS
EVEN MORE IMPORTANT. DAYDREAMING,
NOODLING ABOUT, BEING LOST IN
THOUGHT ARE ALL WORTHY AND
IMPORTANT USES OF YOUR TIME!
DRAWING IS A BIT LIKE
ACTING. TRY AND REALLY
IMAGINE WHAT THE
THING YOU ARE DRAWING
WOULD BE LIKE IF IT
WAS IN FRONT
OF YOU.
DRAWING WELL IS A LONG, LONG JOURNEY THAT YOU NEVER REALLY FINISH.
THERE'S NO POINT WHEN YOU ARE 'READY' YOU JUST NEED TO BE DOING THE
BEST DRAWING YOU CAN DO ON THAT GIVEN DAY.
IF YOU CAN, DRAW EVERY DAY. IT SHOULDN'T BE SOMETHING YOU
SCHEDULE IN LIKE EXERCISE OR HOMEWORK, IT'S JUST SOMETHING YOU
DO WHENEVER YOU HAVE A MOMENT FREE.

MoRE BooKS BY ANDY GRiFFiTHS

Hey, thanks for coming on the adventure with me—I hope you had as much fun as I did. If you'd like to keep the fun going, then here's a guide to some of the many book-based adventures I've created for you. So what are you waiting for?

YOU & ME series
(illustrated by Bill Hope)
A fully illustrated series featuring YOU (the reader) and ME (the narrator) going on ridiculously epic, funny and danger-filled adventures together.

The TREEHOUSE series
(illustrated by Terry Denton)

A series of 13 fully illustrated novels detailing the madcap adventures of Terry (the illustrator) and Andy (the writer) who live in an amazing, ever-growing, ever-more-astonishing treehouse. The series begins with *The 13-Storey Treehouse* and ends with *The 169-Storey Treehouse* (but books can be read and enjoyed in any order). There is also a book of short stories, *Treehouse Tales*, a companion guide to the series, *Who's Who and What's Where in the Treehouse,* two Joke Books and a Bumper Fun Book.

The JUST series
(illustrated by Terry Denton)

Fast-paced, funny short stories narrated by the crazy, stupid, annoying, disgusting and often shocking young Andy. The books feature extensive marginal illustrations and nonsense by Terry Denton. Books: *Just Tricking!, Just Annoying!, Just Stupid!, Just Crazy!, Just Disgusting!, Just Shocking!, Just Macbeth!* and *Just Doomed!*

EARLY READERS
(illustrated by Terry Denton)

These two joyfully silly rhyming books use a phonics-based approach to tell wildly entertaining same-sound stories. Books: *The Big Fat Cow That Went Kapow* and *The Cat on the Mat is Flat*

The BUM Trilogy

The epic Bum Trilogy tells the story of Zack Freeman, his crazy runaway bum, a crack bum-fighting unit called the B-team and some of the biggest, ugliest and meanest bums ever to roam the face of the Earth. Books: *The Day My Bum Went Pyscho, Zombie Bums from Uranus* and *Bumageddon: The Final Pongflict*

The SCHOOLING AROUND series

A set of four novels chronicling the amazing goings-on at Northwest Southeast Central School. Sure to appeal to both confident and emerging readers, they are also ideal for parents and classroom teachers to read aloud. Books: *Treasure Fever!*, *Pencil of Doom!*, *Mascot Madness!* and *Robot Riot!*

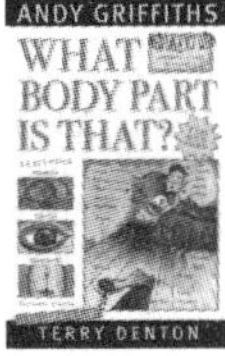

FACT-FREE Guidebooks

(illustrated by Terry Denton)

Two seriously silly, fully illustrated 100% fact-free guidebooks that aim to present as much unscientific data and misinformation as it's possible to cram into two seriously silly, fully illustrated 100% fact-free guidebooks. Books: *What Bumosaur is That?* and *What Body Part is That?*

ONCE UPON A SLIME: 45 Fun Ways to Get Writing ... FAST!

(illustrated by Terry Denton)

Designed for teachers, students and young aspiring writers, the book contains 45 fun writing activities, such as lists, instructions, cartoons, personal stories, poems and pocket books. Examples from Andy's books are used throughout to demonstrate techniques and to inspire readers to have fun playing with ideas, words and pictures.

FRee PRiNTABLE ACTiViTY SHeeTS

The activity sheets listed below are available as copyright-free downloadable PDFs at **andygriffiths.com.au/downloads** and also on the Children's Laureate website (scan the QR code below). **Have fun!**

Activity sheets

A Very Deep Hole (pages 10–11)
Andy's Writing Tips (pages 140–141)
Bill's Drawing Tips (pages 142–143)
Design an Adventure Mobile (pages 6–7)
Design a Monster (pages 86–87)
Open the Box (pages 74–77)
Time Machine (pages 2–4)